PREFACE.

The importance of female culture cannot be too highly estimated, especially in this country, where our institutions depend on the virtue of the people. A self-governed nation must be both intelligent and religious; for if a principle of moral restraint dwells not in the breast of a man, he cannot live peacefully in society, without the terror of some external, constraining force. Society must sink into a state of anarchy, from which a relentless despotism will be evolved, unless it feels the moral force of the sentiment of duty. And on what agency are we to depend for the creation and cultivation of this mighty conservative idea of DUTY, in the teeming millions of our future population? Are our pulpits and our educational appliances sufficient to accomplish this great work? Nay! That they are indispensable and potent instrumentalities, that they cannot be too highly appreciated or earnestly supported, is freely admitted; but there is A POWER BEHIND THE SCHOOL-ROOM AND THE CHURCH, which is capable of neutralizing the efforts of both. Maternal influence, acting on the infant mind in its first stage of impressibility, stamps an almost ineffaceable image of good or evil upon it, long before it can be made to feel the power of the teacher or the minister. Hence the necessity of multiplied, earnest endeavors to promote the growth of the loftiest and holiest traits of mind and heart, in the young women who are destined to be the mothers of a succeeding generation, and, consequently, to exert that fearful influence, which, more than all others, will determine its character. This book is an humble but earnest effort to stimulate and direct the growth of female mind, and thereby to fit it for the fulfilment of its high earthly mission, and for felicity in the world of spirits. If God will be pleased to make it a dew-drop of love, beauty, and fertility in the spirits of some of the daughters of our land, the highest ambition of the author will be satisfied.

D. W.

ELM STREET PARSONAGE,
NEW BEDFORD, Aug. 1851.

CONTENTS.

CHAPTER I.

THE MISTAKE OF A LIFETIME.

CHAPTER II.

THE FOUNTAIN OF LIFE UNSEALED.

CHAPTER III.

INFLUENCE.

CHAPTER IV.

THE TRUE SPHERE OF WOMAN.

CHAPTER V.

LOVELINESS OF SPIRIT.

CHAPTER VI.

SELF-RELIANCE.

CHAPTER IX.

THE YOUNG LADY AT HOME.

CHAPTER X.

THE YOUNG LADY FROM HOME.

CHAPTER XI.

COURTSHIP AND MARRIAGE.

THE

YOUNG LADY'S COUNSELLOR.

CHAPTER I.

THE MISTAKE OF A LIFETIME.

WILL the light-hearted maiden, whose laughing eyes glance at these lines, permit her attention to rest a moment or two upon the sketch I am about to pencil? albeit, it may be of a more sad and sombre hue than the bright images usually floating before her imagination. Behold, then, a once puissant lady struggling with the agonies of life's last hours! She is rich in gold and diamonds, in palaces and lands. The blast of her war-trumpets can summon squadrons of armed men to the field. Her word of command can cover the seas with the white sails of one of the proudest navies of the globe. Her red-cross banner floats in pride from many a "castled crag," and over

"A land of beauty
Fondled by the circling sea."

Yet is the face of this queenly sufferer deadly pale; her eyes are wandering and restless; and her expressive features indicate extreme mental distress. Legions of sad remembrances are marching through her mind, terrible as a phantom army to her fears. A mitred prelate stands beside her royal couch, vainly endeavoring, by his devotions, to soothe her ruffled spirit, and fit it for its passage to the veiled world beyond. Vain attempt! Every look of England's royal mistress, the great ELIZABETH, that once haughty daughter of the Tudors, seems to say: "Gladly would I surrender pomp, power, and empire, for the sweet innocency of childhood; for

'A conscience free from sin!'"

And thus, with her spirit tossed upon a sea of doubt, restless and shuddering, she surrenders her earthly throne, and stands undistinguished amidst a crowd of spirits, a trembling subject at the bar of the King of kings!

This is a spectacle of sadness. Such sorrow, in such a mind, at such an hour, was very painful to endure. Nevertheless, it was only the necessary sequence of *a great and fatal mistake* which had ruled the life of the queen. What was that mistake? She had relied upon things *external to herself* for enjoyment and content! She had looked to her crown, her kingdom, her friends, as springs from which streams of pleasure were to flow into her soul. She had dreamed of attaining happiness by levying contributions upon the vast array of outward and visible objects which the Providence of God had placed within her reach. Vain expectation! Illusive dream! It made her life turbulent and uneasy, and her death painful and unsatisfactory. She had obviously mistaken the false for the true, — the evil for the good. Failing to discern the true "*fountain of living water*," she lived and died in the vain attempt to quench the mighty thirst of her undying spirit at "cisterns," which, though of imposing magnificence and peerless splendor, nevertheless "*held no water!*"

I am seriously inclined to fear that the young lady to whom I now write is entering the great temple of life under the guidance of this same fatal mistake. Is it not so, my reader? Are you not looking out upon the thousand gay things of life with the expectation of deriving your choicest pleasure from their possession? Is not life vocal to your ears with alluring sounds of invitation to partake of its delights and be happy? And do you not listen to those voices with pleasing rapture, and fancy how completely blessed you should be, if wealth to purchase admission to the halls of gayety and fashion were yours? If you were the "belle" of the ball-room, the fascination of the soirée, the "admired of all admirers" at Newport or Saratoga, the betrothed of some noble-minded lover, or the wife of some doting husband, then, you imagine, your heart would throb with genuine and substantial bliss. The desire which, by its restlessness, now keeps you from true mental repose, would then, you fancy, be satisfied: that sense of soul-emptiness of which you are so painfully conscious would be removed, and you be the delighted possessor of genuine bliss on earth. These things being so, are you not self-convicted of the same error whose disastrous consequences you just now beheld in my picture of the royal Elizabeth? That fatal mistake, of looking wholly to things external to herself for happiness, which embittered her life and robbed her death-bed of all true comfort, is already beguiling you. That mistake must be corrected, or you will also live unblessed, and die uncomforted.

Let us enter, at least in fancy, yon ancient house, whose high-peaked roofs and gable ends proclaim it a relic of the "days that are no more." Within, it is desolate and lonely. A venerable lady of the olden time is housekeeper; and a girl of rude manners, but robust frame, is her servant. Let us ascend these rickety stairs, and introduce ourselves to the owner of this antiquated pile. Here is his room. It is a laboratory, containing, as you may see, a vast array of bottles filled with chemicals, and piles of musty folios. Bending over his alembic with fixed attention, behold the philosopher himself, wrapped in the folds of a huge dressing-gown, and a high study-cap upon his head. Gray ringlets steal down upon his shoulders. His studious face is covered with deep wrinkles; for sixty years he has steadily experimented by day and dreamed at night, in the vain hope of wringing from nature a mighty secret. Profoundly, and with unwearied patience, he has interrogated nature, and bent over that alembic and its mysterious mixtures, until the manly vigor of previous years has given way to the decrepitude of trembling age. Still he toils and will toil on, until he falls, a martyr to his theory, into the dreary grave. And for what? you inquire. Lady! he is an alchemist. He seeks the philosopher's stone by which all baser metals are to be transmuted into gold; and the elixir of life, by which all diseases are to be cured, and our race endowed with eternal youth!

"Philosopher's stone, indeed! Elixir of life!

What nonsense! That old alchemist, with all his philosophical learning, must be sadly lacking in common sense!" you vehemently exclaim, your pursed brow and flashing eyes expressing also the earnestness of your indignation at his folly.

But why should *you*, young madam, be so incensed against that harmless old alchemist, while you are guilty of a folly equally obvious, but infinitely more serious in its consequences? Why is that theorist a fool? Simply because he seeks an obvious impossibility: he pursues a dream, — he grasps a shadow! You do the same; for have I not convicted you, on the testimony of your own consciousness, of seeking to extract true happiness from the external world alone? With equal discretion might you search after the elixir of life, or the philosopher's stone. For how can perishing matter satisfy imperishable mind? Can a mind like yours, endowed with cravings after the Divine, the infinite, and the immortal, be satisfied with the finite, the created, the ever-changing visible world? Never! It is impossible, in the nature of things. And a mind unsatisfied is a mind unhappy.

Listen to the sad song of a poet, who dipped his pen in an inkhorn filled with tears of bitter disappointment, and, writing from his own history, said:

"As charm on charm unwinds
Which robed our idols, and we see too sure
Nor worth nor beauty dwells from out the mind's
Ideal shape of such: yet still it binds
The fatal spell, and still it draws us on,
Reaping the whirlwind from the oft-sown winds;
The stubborn heart, its alchemy begun,
Seems ever near the prize—wealthiest when most undone."

There never was a mind, since the world began, which would not have sadly responded to the truth of these lines, after a thorough trial of the power of the external world to bless the heart. And to universal experience is superadded the emphatic declaration of Jehovah, who has written, with his own fingers, on the arch which spans the great entrance to real life, this significant inquiry, "*Wherefore do you spend money for that which is not bread? and your labor for that which satisfieth not?*"

Pause, young lady, in presence of this Divine question, and this universal experience! Permit your mind to reflect gravely on the imminent risk, not to say daring recklessness, of venturing into a sea where every previous voyager has wrecked his bark, and where so many have perished. Let the combined voices of God and man settle the question for you, without making the dangerous trial yourself. Receive it as a mental conviction, that, although external objects may please for a moment, as toys amuse children, — although, in their appropriate uses, they may swell the fountain of the mind's joy, — yet they are necessarily and immutably unfitted to be its portion.

Should you, my dear reader, concur with me in this opinion, you will have taken the first step toward escaping from the fatal mistake which spoiled the life of the royal Elizabeth.

"From whence, then, am I to derive true happiness? If it is so fatal to look for it to things *without* myself, whither shall I look?" you very properly and eagerly inquire.

. will permit a human and a Divine teacher to solve your problem. The former is a poet. He says:

"There are, in this loud stormy tide
Of human care and crime,
With whom the melodies abide
Of the everlasting chime;
Who *carry music in their hearts.*
Through dusky lane and wrangling mart
Plying their daily task with busier feet,
Because their secret souls a holy strain repeat."

The latter, speaking under heavenly inspiration, writes that "*a good man shall be satisfied from himself.*" Both passages teach that the sources of genuine pleasure are to be sought *within the mind itself:* that the rich repose enjoyed by a happy mind originates from something dwelling within itself: that happiness does not flow in from the outer world, but springs up, unseen by others, within the mysterious sanctuary of the soul: and that the power of visible things to swell the tide of harmony in the mind depends upon the mind itself. The everlasting chime of melody, which may charm the ear of her who listens aright to the voices of the visible world, originates in the soul of the listener. Whoso would draw a "concord of sweet sounds" from the world without, must carry music in her heart; just as the maiden, who sits before the richly-toned instrument, must first have the musical idea in herself, before she can call forth floods of melody from its obedient keys.

As Schiller justly inquires,

> "Doth the harmony
> In the sweet lute-strings belong
> To the purchaser, who, dull of ear, doth keep
> The instrument? True she hath bought the right
> To strike it into fragments — yet no art
> To wake its silvery tones, and melt with bliss
> Of thrilling song! Truth for the wise exists,
> And beauty for the feeling heart."

The flower blooms brightly, and exhales odoriferous perfume to myriads of insects; but the industrious bee, taught by its curious instinct, alone extracts and stores away its delicious sweets. So, though the earth contains ten thousand flowers, whose bloom may delight the soul, and whose odor may ravish the heart, yet those alone whose minds are fitly disposed can enjoy the luxury. Outward things are to the mind just what the mind is to itself. If the mind be its own heaven, then is earth its Eden; but if it be its own hell, then the things and objects of life are instruments of vexation and of torture.

Within the mind itself, therefore, the elixir of life must be produced. The human bosom is the little chamber in which, as in a laboratory, bliss or woe is created. There we must study the occult art of extracting honey from the world's flowers, music from its motions, and enjoyment from its relations. There we must obtain strength to subdue it to our service. There we must acquire the alchemy of transmuting its poisons into nutritious sweets. There must we look, and there find, if we find it at all, the fountain of a joyous life—of all true pleasure. "*The kingdom of God is* WITHIN YOU," said the Lord Jesus; and so of a happy life,—its springs are WITHIN YOU.

A lordly poet once stood amidst a fearful storm, at night, on the Alps. Nature, in one of her most savage aspects, in one of her most appalling moments, stood before him. The scene was sufficiently dreadful to send the blood back to the stoutest heart, and to hush even a courageous mind to trembling reverence. But there stood the poet, in a rapture of delight, which he expressed in these beautiful lines:

> "O night
> And storm and darkness, ye are wondrous strong,—
> Yet lovely in your strength, as is the light
> Of a dark eye in woman!—far along,
> From peak to peak, the rattling crags among,
> Leaps the live thunder!—not from one lone cloud,
> But every mountain now hath found a tongue,
> And Jura answers, through her misty shroud,
> Back to the joyous Alps, who call to her aloud!
> *   *   *   *   *   *
> How the lit lake shines a phosphoric sea,
> And the big rain comes dancing to the earth!
> And now again 't is black, and now the glee
> Of the loud hills shakes with its mountain mirth,
> As if they did rejoice o'er a young earthquake's birth."

Whence the enthusiastic pleasure, worthy of the spirits of the storm, which inspired these verses? Why should this poet revel, as in a fairy-land of beauty, over a scene which caused his companions to tremble? Why should the same occurrence pro duce precisely opposite effects on the different spectators? Whence the difference? Plainly in the minds of the spectators only. The poet, nurtured among the most rugged scenes of nature and reckless of all danger, had a soul in harmony with the storm, and could enjoy its terrors; while others, unable to perceive the sublime and beautiful, through fear of the terrible which surrounded it, beheld and trembled. A striking illustration this, you now perceive, of the truth, that things without the mind bless or curse it only as that mind is predisposed. If fearful, and alive only to the terrible, it will tremble; if bold, and sensitive to what is sublime and beautiful, it will be delighted.

The mind has a similar power to determine the influence which its condition in social life shall exert upon it. The most abject poverty cannot compel it to be unhappy; the most favorable state in life cannot insure its pleasure. Upon itself alone depends the power of circumstance to embitter or to charm. Let it be at peace with itself, loving the pure and lovely, living on rational and cheerful hopes, and, as the poet said of a mind animated by hope,

> "Hope, — the sweet bird, — while *that* the air can fill,
> Let earth be ice — the soul has summer still."

Are you in doubt concerning the possibility of

maintaining a summer of warmth and beauty in the soul, while the desolation of a Greenland winter reigns around? Let me remove your scepticism by portraying an illustrative fact. Enter with me the chamber of a sick and suffering maiden. Observe, as you cross the threshold, its utter barrenness of all that ministers to taste or comfort. How bare its cracked and smoky walls! No carpet covers the uneven floor, — no couches or easy-chairs invite to repose. A chair or two, a rude bed, whose well-patched covering eloquently proclaims the dominion of poverty, compose its entire furniture. But see! How pale is the face of that young sufferer! Listen to her suppressed groans — to her piercing shriek! Her convulsive starts, her distorted features, alarm you. "Poor creature! How she suffers!" is your involuntary exclamation. But she grows more calm, for the paroxysm is over. Now, mark the lovely serenity which steals over and settles upon her countenance! With what a radiant smile of welcome she greets you! How heavenly is the expression of her now lustrous eyes! How rich in sublime sentiment are the words which flow from her thin lips! What ardent love, what holy submission, what lofty spiritual ecstasy, she professes! As you listen you are astonished, and in an inward whisper exclaim, 'What a happy creature!"

Yes, she is happy; for this is no ideal picture, but a faithful likeness of an actual sufferer. For a series of years, this dear girl was tormented by violent convulsions, which, occurring every few hours, dislocated her joints, and caused an unimaginable amount of physical agony. Yet, through it all, her unrepining spirit triumphed in God. With heroic constancy she endured her unexampled sufferings; and maintained an intercourse with God so elevated and sublime, that her joys were more unspeakable than her sufferings. If her physical life was literally full of anguish, her spiritual life was full of glory! Her "earth was ice," but her "soul had summer still."

In contrast with this painting of strong light and deep shadow, permit me to place another, as sketched by the brilliant pen of a poet. It is that of minds surrounded by gayety and music, yet miserable in the last degree:

> "But midst the throng, in merry masquerade,
> Lurk there no hearts that throb with secret pain,
> E'en through the closest cerement half betrayed?
> * * * * * *
> To such the gladness of the gamesome crowd
> Is source of wayward thought and stern disdain;
> How do they loathe the laughter idly loud,
> And long to change the robe of revel for the shroud!"

Here you behold persons not only rejecting what is pleasurable and joyous in a scene of revelry, but actually busy at extracting torture from them. They stand in a circle whose splendid gayety is adapted to bewitch the senses, while jocund laughter and mirth-inspiring music ring in their ears, with their hearts throbbing with keenest anguish, loathing the spectacle, and blindly longing for the solitude of the grave.

Pray, tell me, lady, why the maiden was happy under circumstances so adverse and painful, while these inmates of the hall of pleasure were the victims of exquisite misery? The former, though in physical torture and poverty, enjoyed a mental heaven; the latter, though in an external Eden, suffered a mental hell. Why this difference? Plainly because, as we have before affirmed, the mind is its own heaven or its own hell; and because, if pleasure reigns not within the breast, it cannot come from without: while, if it is queen within, outward things may disturb, but cannot destroy its reign. How consummate, therefore, is the folly of *looking out of the mind* for your enjoyment! How wise and prudent to look within yourself for that happiness which is at once your aspiration and your privilege!

The truth unfolded and amplified in this chapter may seem so trivial to my reader, that she may be disposed to toss her little head, and throw down my book in proud disdain. She can hardly persuade herself that the difference between looking within or without herself for happiness is so great that to do the latter would be a *fatal* mistake. But let me assure her that

"Things are not what they seem;"

That little seeming differences often involve almost

infinite consequences; that it is the part of wisdom to look well at those truths which the heart despises, remembering that

> "The poor herb, when all that pomp could bring
> Were vain to charm, admits to Oberon's ring;"

and that a little scorn at little things may blast your brightest hopes, and tumble your most magnificent expectations to the dust. It was thus that an ancient prince of Sardinia lost his own liberty and his friend's life. He had fallen, by the chance of war, into the prison of Bologna. ASINELLI, his friend, contrived a plan for his escape. He had him enclosed in an empty tun which had contained wine. Trusty friends were waiting, with swift horses, outside the city. The tun was being borne along the passages of the prison. It reached the gates unsuspected, when a soldier observed a lock of hair protruding from the barrel; it was opened, and the unhappy prince remanded to his dungeon. Asinelli was banished, and another friend was put to death. Thus the trifling neglect to conceal a lock of hair cost years of sorrow to many hearts. Perhaps the men who closed the barrel saw that lock of hair, as you see this truth; and perhaps they thought, in their haste, it was hardly worth while to hinder themselves by stopping to enclose it. If so, how fatal their haste! It undid their labors, and ruined their plan. Even so, my dear young friend, a hasty contempt for the counsel which teaches you that "earth's real wealth is *in* the heart," and assures you that to rely on outward things for happiness is a fatal mistake, may be ruinous to all that is really precious in your life and destiny. Receive it, therefore, with reflection; follow it with resolution; adhere to it with determination. Then shall you esca[illegible] the experience of an earthly mind, wh[illegible]rote, in the bitterness of his disappoin[illegible]t, that

> "Dark t[illegible]hood grows the heaven that smiled
> [illegible]n the clear vision nature gave the child."

CHAPTER II.

THE FOUNTAIN OF LIFE UNSEALED.

UPON the loftiest and most rugged peaks of the Alps, a species of fir-tree is said to flourish among rocks whose almost utter destitution of soil refuses support to plant or flower. Yet there this pine-tree grows, defying the barren soil and the "howling tempests,"

> "Till its height and frame
> Are worthy of the mountains from whose blocks
> Of bleak gray granite into life it came,
> And grew a giant tree."

Whence is the life of this gigantic tree supported? The scanty soil, in which its straggling roots scarcely find a covering, is obviously insufficient. Is it, then, self-supported? Does its nutriment arise from itself alone? Nay, for we can hardly conceive how a stripling fir could wax into a "giant tree," without obtaining the materials of its growth from some source besides itself. Hence we infer, that, while its roots exhaust the little nutriment contained in the soil, its branches embrace and absorb the atmosphere; and, by an invisible process of almost infinite skill, the tree elaborates the elements of life from its particles. Thus, while its growth and greatness may be said to be from within itself, yet are they not wholly of itself.

"The mind may do the same." It may enjoy its healthiest and highest life amidst the most rugged features of external existence; for, like the Alpine fir, it may find invisible elements of support, which, though not originating in itself, nevertheless spring up within it as from a fountain of living rapture. If left wholly dependent upon itself, it could not find real enjoyment in an Eden of beauty; for, in fallen human nature, happiness is not an inborn spring; it is a living fountain, brought into the heart by a power which, though dwelling in the temple of the soul, is not of it, but infinitely above it.

Nor is it possible to attain real enjoyment without

the presence of this power. In the preceding chapter I have shown that no height of intellectual greatness, no elevation of social condition, no amount of terrestrial wealth, no softness of climate, no beauty of landscape, — nay, nor all human things combined, — can, of themselves, enable the unassisted heart to discourse sweet music, or attain to blissful tranquillity. Yet I cannot forbear to fortify this vital point by another striking example. Hear the confessions of a wealthy peer of England, — a scholar, a poet, a traveller, a man in whom every visible condition of human happiness met, — and learn the total insufficiency of all to cheer the spirit; yea, learn how desolate a thing is the human heart, when it proudly leans upon itself alone, in the following melancholy language, which this "poor rich man" addressed to his sister:

"I was disposed to be pleased. I am a lover of nature and an admirer of beauty. I can bear fatigue and welcome privation, and have seen some of the noblest views in the world. But in all this, the recollection of bitterness, and more especially of recent and home desolation, which must accompany me through life, has preyed upon me here; and neither the music of the shepherds, the crashing of the avalanche, nor the torrent, the mountain, the glacier, the forest, nor the cloud, have for one moment lightened the weight upon my heart, nor enabled me to lose my own wretched identity in the majesty and the power and glory around, above and beneath me."

If this sad lament of a weary heart were a solitary fact in human history, it would not be admissible to infer a general principle from it. But it is not. Every soul that has trusted to itself alone, since the world began, has uttered a corresponding wail of agony; and it is therefore a fair example of what the human mind is, when left to its own resources, — a miserable, empty, wretched thing. Miss LANDON'S harp gave forth a note of truth when it sang

"The heart is made too sensitive
Life's daily pain to bear;
It beats in music, but it beats
Beneath a deep despair."

What, then, is the sacred source of true and lasting bliss? What is that which must be brought into the mind to give genuine enjoyment? If my young friend will humbly take her seat where the beautiful Mary sat, she shall be taught the mighty secret, in words of authority, from the lips of Jesus. He says: "*Whosoever drinketh of the water that I shall give him shall never thirst; but the water that I shall give him* SHALL BE IN HIM *a well of water, springing up into eternal life.*"

"*If a man love me, he will keep my words; and my Father will love him, and we will come unto him and make our abode with him.*"

"*I will see you again, and your heart shall rejoice, and your joy no man taketh from you.*"

"*My peace give I unto you.*"

Here, then, my beloved reader, the great truth stands out before you. God received *into* the soul by simple faith, is the grand and only source of true happiness. He is that fountain of living water, whose streams refresh the weary spirit, and satisfy its immortal thirst. Where he dwells there abide peace, love, joy and hope, in all their beauty: the storms of passion arise not in His presence. The visible world, gilded by the rays of His glory, can be really and innocently enjoyed, because he brings the inter nal faculties into harmony with external things. The relations of social life can be enjoyed; their duties performed with efficiency and pleasure. The future is invested with grandeur and glory. All the interests of life are felt to be safe, for they are in the keeping of God, — of God not afar off in clouds and darkness, but of God abiding in perpetual spiritual manifestation within the breast. The beautiful ideal of the Grecian mythology, concerning the goddess whose soft and delicate tread caused the green herb and lovely flower to spring up on the island of Cyprus, becomes a literal fact in the experience of a christian lady; for, in whatever soul God enters a welcomed guest, every lovely plant springs up, and every beauteous flower grows with divine fertility. He is "*a well of water springing up into eternal life.*"

Can you conceive of any calamity more appalling

than a widely-spread famine? How terrible the idea, even to the fancy, of a whole nation cut off from its resources by universal sterility! But how much more so must be the fact itself! With what fearful eagerness the people watch for signs of rain! Yet weeks, months and years pass, and the sky is clear and cloudless; the sun glows fiercely in the heavens; the air is hot and sultry; the earth is parched and cracked; every blade of grass, every herb and every tree, dries up, until all is arid and barren as the desert. Nature languishes, and in her feebleness oppresses her children, until disease and groaning fill the land, and hecatombs of dead cover its surface with graves.

Yet, in the certain prospect of such an event, behold the sublime serenity of the Egyptian nation in the age of Joseph. The face of the people is gay and cheerful. The voice of song resounds all over the land, from the hundred gates of Thebes to the mouths of the Nile. Though the nation was assured that for seven years the sway of this terrible evil would be maintained, yet a most absolute fearlessness of death kept every heart strong, and excluded all apprehension of serious suffering, alike from the proud palaces of Pharaoh and the mud hovel of the peasant. Famine reigned in the land, yet peace dwelt in the hearts of the people.

Whence arose this astonishing national repose in the midst of so menacing an evil? Behold the immense stores of food with which the vast granaries of the land are groaning! And, at the head of the government, behold the inspired man whose prophetic wisdom foretold the event,—whose forecast prepared these almost boundless supplies, and whose wisdom presides over their distribution! These facts explain the great enigma of so much calmness amid so much that was formidable! The people knew their inability to cope with the sterility of nature, but their reliance on the predictions and ability of Joseph was so strong they could not fear. Famine might rage,—they were helpless to resist it; but Joseph had provided an ample supply for their wants, and they rejoiced in a happy consciousness of security from starvation and death.

You have no difficulty, my young reader, in understanding the action of this confidence in the minds of the Egyptians, and that without it they would have been absolutely wretched. It will therefore be easy for you to transfer the idea to your own necessities and resources. Viewing yourself in your relations to human society, you cannot fail to perceive much of evil, of danger, and of suffering, before you. You everywhere behold women whose early career was as gay, as secure, as promising, as your own, the victims of heart desolation, of acute suffering, of neglect, of poverty, — to whom life is as a desert waste, where suffocating winds sweep rudely past them, and stifling sands threaten to bury them in death. In one direction, you see a daughter thrown upon her own resources by the premature death of her parents; in another, a wife, but yesterday a happy bride, left to indescribable sorrow by the neglect of an unfaithful husband, or plunged into a mournful widowhood by the visitation of death. What multitudes of women, who, a little while ago, rejoiced as gayly as the joyous lark in the thoughtlessness of a happy girlhood, are living in weakness, toil and sadness, weary of life, yet unwilling and unfit to die! True, much of this vast amount of female misery might have been avoided; yet, in the full knowledge of its existence and of your own weakness, you cannot avoid the conviction that you are liable to similar experiences. With the Egyptians you can see dark forms of *evil* thronging your path. You dare not face them alone! They are calculated to affright your spirit. What, then, is necessary to give you an intelligent and stable peace of mind? What to save you from these sufferings and sorrows of your sex? Plainly, you need a *confidence* like that of the Egyptians. Your heart must rely upon some power, able and willing to preserve you from such manifest evils. A friend, who will guide your steps, watch over and secure your interests, support you in your trials, and deliver you in trouble, is a necessity of your nature. Could you be sure of such a friend, you could gaze upon the ills of life with as fearless a smile as that with which the people of Pharaoh looked upon the sterility of their country.

But where is the human friend whose qualities are such as to inspire you with this essential confidence? Alas! he is not to be found; for every other mortal is like yourself exposed to trouble and danger. If it were otherwise, — if that venerable parent who has watched your infancy and youth with so much solicitude, and in whose love you feel so secure, possessed the *power* to protect you through life,—you know that the thread on which his existence hangs is more frail than a lute-string. How, then, can you calmly face your destiny with such a trust? You cannot do it! You need power, wisdom, love, sympathy, duration, in the Being on whom your spirit can repose in perfect serenity. And who is such a friend but Jehovah? Whose friendship can calm your soul but his? What but religious faith can inspire so delightful a trust? What is there in the human soul to create this sense of safety, amidst the unquestionable dangers by which it is surrounded? Nothing! positively nothing! Self-reliance is presumptuous arrogance. To trust in man is to pluck the fruit that grows on "folly's topmost twig." To be without confidence is to be wretched, whether your home be the palace of a merchant prince, or the cottage of a toiling peasant. To a religious faith, therefore, are you shut up. The point before you is as plain as a self-evident truth; you must be wretched or religious. Embrace the faith of Christ, and forthwith a confidence will spring up in your soul which will disarm life of its terrors, enable you to defy its emergencies, assure you that all chance is excluded from the government of the world, that your interests are all safe in the hands of the infinite God, whose attributes are pledged to promote your safety. You will then see Omnipotence as the wall built around you; infinite resources ready to be employed in your behalf, and boundless love distributing the mercies requisite to supply your necessities.

Blessed with this sublime trust, you will walk the ways of life as calmly as the ideal pilgrim, in the picture of a German artist, whose beautiful painting contained a lovely child walking slowly along a narrow path, bounded on each side by a terrific precipice, the edges of which were concealed from him by a luxuriant border of fruits and flowers. Behind this infant pilgrim there stood an angel, his white wings spreading upward into the evening sky, his hands placed lightly on the shoulders of the little traveller, as if to guide him safely along the dangerous path. The child's eyes were closed, that the beautiful flowers and luscious fruit might not tempt him to pause or step aside; and he walked calmly forward, smiling ineffable content, as if perfectly satisfied, so long as he felt the gentle pressure of those angelic hands. With religious faith you may walk through the evils of life equally fearless, safe and happy.

Nor is the influence of a religious faith on the fears of the heart its only relation to your present enjoyment. It is peculiarly adapted to that comparative isolation from active life which falls to the lot of your sex. Home is woman's world, as well as her empire. Man lives more in society. The busy marts of trade, the bustling exchange, the activity of artisan life, are his spheres. They call forth his energies, and occupy his thoughts. But woman's life is spent in comparative solitude. She is, therefore, if possible, more dependent upon her inward resources than her more stirring companion. And how is she to feel contented with the loneliness of her lot, in spite of that "longing for sympathy that belongs to her nature"? She cannot be, unless she enjoys the supports of religion. But, with this divine life within her, she becomes, to use the language of the Duchess of Newcastle, "a beautiful creature, tremblingly alive to the influences of this beautiful world, tremblingly conscious that but a thin veil separates this actual daily life from the world of spirits. A being with whom the sense of immortality is an actual presence, lingering about her bed and about her path, and whose heart is cheered as by the breathings of the air of paradise. Such a being as this, finding herself unguided and alone among those of her sex whose talk is of Paris fashions, bonnets and balls, — whose lives are worthy of their conversation, — such a being can lean on no earthly arm for support, nor look to any earthly sympathy for comfort. Over her heart God must breathe the holy calm of his peace."

And sweet is the calm he breathes, — rich and exuberant the joy he inspires. While "worldly women are poor, suffering ones, who wander in the thorny paths of life, pining for happiness and going astray after its very shadow," religious women find an "unspeakable joy" in religion, which enriches every inferior and earthly pleasure. To them "there is joy in feeling the first breath of the morning fanning the cheek; joy in the balm of April sunshine and showers, and in the flowers of beautiful May. There is joy in the joyous laugh and the silvery voice of childhood,— in the romance of youth ere care shades her heart; there is joy in the breast of the bride as she gives 'her hand, with her heart in it,' to her lover; joy in a mother's bosom as she presses her first-born to her breast. Yes, even earth has its joys; but, alas! they are as fleeting as sunshine, as perishable as flowers; but they have also a joy deeper, fuller, richer, sweeter, imperishable as the undying spirit, — it is the joy of religious love." How desirable is this joy to you, my dear young lady, whose life, in common with that of most of your sex, must necessarily be spent in comparative isolation!

In some portions of the frigid zones the inhabitants provide themselves with habitations beneath the surface of the ground. During their brief summer, they convey large stores of food and fuel to these subterranean abodes. When winter comes, they enter them and live peacefully there, indifferent to the desolating storms and dreary snows which fall and rage above their heads. Their home is their winter world, and it contains all their little wants demand. Hence, they live in secure plenty, smiling at the howling storm which leaves their abode untouched and safe.

Very similar is the influence of religion in human life. It makes its possessor independent of outward circumstances; it enables her to defy the changes of life. What if friends are false, health decays, fortune fails, wasting storms drive furiously around her head? Is her happiness lost? Nay! for she has not depended upon friends, health or fortune, for her highest pleasure. As superior streams of comfort she has welcomed and enjoyed them, but not as the fountain of her delight. Their removal, therefore, leaves her in full possession of her chief good. A sterile, snowy winter may rage without, but she has her God within herself, and is satisfied. He is her world. His presence and favor constitute her heaven, though her visible life is filled with discomfort and woe. Very strongly, yet very beautifully, did an ancient Christian, according to TAULERIUS, once express this divine bliss, when a doubting friend inquired, "What would you do, if God should cast you into hell?"

"Cast me into hell! God will not do that. But if he were to cast me into hell, I have two arms, — an arm of faith and an arm of love; with these I would lay hold on God, and cling to him so firmly that I would take him with me! And surely no evil could befall me there; for, I would rather be with God in hell, than to be in heaven without him!"

This is very strong — perhaps too strong — language; yet it nobly expresses the superiority of the Christian to adverse circumstances, — his independence of human events and troubles. The old poet, VAUGHN, has a stanza which is so instinct with this spirit of heroic triumph over outward vicissitudes, I cannot forbear quoting it. Viewing the Christian in an era of persecution and martyrdom, he puts these burning words into his lips:

"Burn me alive with curious skilful pain,
Cut up and search each warm and breathing vein;
When all is done, death brings a quick release,
And the poor mangled body sleeps in peace.
Hale me to prisons, shut me up in brass,
My still free soul from thence to God shall pass;
Banish or bind me, I can be nowhere
A stranger or alone, — my God is there.
I fear not famine. How can he be said
To starve, who feeds upon the living bread?
And yet this courage springs not from my store, —
Christ gave it me, who can give much more."

How desirable, in a world so changeful as this, that a young lady, so feeble and so exposed, should possess this hidden peace from Christ, which neither creature nor circumstance can take from her!

Perhaps, lady, you are a lover of music. The piano is your favorite instrument, from whose keys you draw many pleasant sounds. Permit me to give you a lesson upon it. You know it contains many wires, all of which are called into use at times, and are necessary to its perfection. Each of these wires has its own peculiar sound, which it must render precisely, else a discord jars on your ear, and destroys the harmony of the music. To create and to preserve this harmony, it has to be submitted to the skilful hand and ear of the tuner; otherwise, as a musical instrument, it would fail to afford you pleasure. However costly in its materials and magnificent in its external finish, you would only be pained by its presence, so long as its tuneless state forbade you to touch a key. But, once in perfect tune, you enjoy exquisite delight, as its delicious melody fills your enraptured ear.

It is thus with your mind. It has various functions and qualities, intellectual and moral, each of which is designed to act in a specific manner; and which *must* so act, to constitute you happy in yourself, and an instrument of good to society. But, like the piano, the mind is out of tune. Though intensely pained by the discords it utters, it nevertheless continually produces them. It requires tuning, therefore, or it must be a self-tormenting thing of discords forever—magnificent in its construction, glorious in its powers, yet failing to attain the sublime end of its creation. To drop my comparison, the mind is unable of itself to develop those qualities which are necessary to its own enjoyment, and to its right influence over others. And nothing less than the power of religion can repress its evil tendencies, and develop its superior qualities. As the tuner of instruments may justly say of the piano, "without me it is nothing," so does Christ actually say to you, lady, "without me ye can do nothing." Christ, and Christ alone, is sufficient to clothe you with that loveliness of moral character which will cause your life to pass happily to yourself and to be beneficial to others. How else can your life be

> "A sacred stream,
> In whose calm depths the beautiful and pure
> Alone are mirrored"?

How else can you acquire that guileless ingenu

ousness, that dignity combined with tenderness, that prudent reserve unmixed with haughtiness, that calm patriotism so modest and yet so heroic, that courage without fierceness, that energy without rashness, that purity without a spot, that earnest self-denying industry, that wise forecast, that prudent economy, that constellation of high moral qualities, whose mild light sweetly gilds the gloom of external circumstances, and makes woman a "spotless form of beauty," — arms her with power to move the soul, to win the affections, to attain the ideal excellence of SCHILLER'S QUEEN ELIZABETH OF SPAIN, who moved

> "With inborn and unboastful majesty,
> Alike from careless levity remote
> And a behavior schooled by selfish rules,
> Alike removed from rashness and from fear.
> With firm and fearless step she ever walked
> The narrow path of duty — all unconscious
> That she won worship, where she never dreamed
> Of approbation"?

Qualities like these can grow to harmonious perfection by nothing less than God in your soul. Their semblances may be produced by simple self-culture; but they will be only as jewels of paste, compared with genuine stones. His presence will adorn you with genuine excellence, render you independent of life's changing joys, satisfy you, and enable you to extract what of pure pleasure exists in earthly things. Thus may your life pass,

> "That every hour
> Shall die as dies a natural flower—
> A self-reviving thing of power;
> That every thought and every deed
> May hold within itself the seed
> Of future good and future need."

CHAPTER III.

INFLUENCE.

"GATHER UP MY INFLUENCE, AND BURY IT WITH ME!" exclaimed a youth, whose unforgiven spirit was sinking into the invisible world. Idle request! Had he begged his friends to bind the free winds, to chain the wild waves, to grasp the fierce lightning, or make a path for the sand-blast, his wish would have been more feasible; for past influence is unchangeable. The sceptical thought that fell as a seed of evil from the lip and grew in the heart of the listener into defiant infidelity, the light word that pierced the spirit like a poisoned dart, the angry glance which stirred the soul to anguish and made tears flow at the midnight hour, are alike beyond our reach. The mind thus wounded sighs on, and after we are dead the chords vibrate which our fingers touched. The measure of that influence, for weal or woe, will lie hidden, a terrible secret, until the day when the spirit, blindly driven to despair and guilt, or blasted by sceptical thought, shall stand writhing and wretched to confront those by whom the offence came, and to teach that *influence is immutable and eternal!*

Such are the fearful sentiments contained in a fugitive poem which once met my eye. They are thoughts peculiarly adapted to the consideration of a young lady; for, whatever may be her grade in society, her talents or opportunities, it is a necessary condition of her existence that she *must* exert this potential thing we call influence. It is not a matter of choice. She cannot say she will not exercise it, for she must. From every glance of her eye, every word of her lips, every act of her life, there goes forth, in a greater or less degree, an invisible power, which produces an effect upon the minds around her. This power to affect others is influence. It is a gift of Heaven to every human being. Whether it shall be productive of evil or good, is for each possessor to determine. It is like the rod of Moses, which was either the prolific instrument of plague and woe, or the means of driving evil and destruction from the land, as the inspired will of its great owner determined. Thus with this precious gift. It may scatter pestilence, desolation and death, or it may bring forth life and beauty; it may be a harp of sweetest melody, making glad the heart of the world, or it may be a discordant trumpet, rousing the passions of mankind to angry and tempestuous strife, as its possessor may decide.

Will you imagine yourself in one of the vast cathedrals of Europe? Behold its spacious aisles and lofty galleries, crowded with masses of spectators of all ranks and of every age, from the gray bearded patriarch of eighty to the fawn-like girl of five or six. Suppose yourself placed before the keys of its magnificent organ, and required to execute a piece of music, with the information that certain keys, bearing particular marks, have the power, if improperly touched, of producing violent pains in the audience, which no medical science could assuage or cure; while, if they are skilfully touched, their delightful melody will create the most exquisite sensations of enduring pleasure. In such a position, would you not exert your utmost powers to avoid those movements which would thrill your auditory with anguish? Would you not enter, with grave earnestness, upon those which would be followed with bursts of joy? Your ardent response is in your heart and eye; and you almost wish for the opportunity of choosing between such alternatives.

If my previous remarks are true, you have not only such an opportunity, but one of far higher and nobler character. By a proper use of this more than fairy gift of influence, you can call into existence emotions of pure delight, capable of infinite self-multiplication in the multitude of human spirits which will come within your sphere during your lifetime. By neglecting the proper use of your gift, you will create agonies of equal duration and intensity. Can you, therefore, refuse a few moments of grave thoughtfulness to so weighty a point? What if life is young, and its paths are strewed with flowers? What if the current of your ordinary ideas runs in a contrary direction? What if a due sense of the true responsibilities of life should restrain, in some degree, the gayety of your spirits? Are you, therefore, to trample upon the happiness of others? Are you to peril your own best interests? Remember, as is your influence, so is your destiny. There is a woe for those who suffer from evil influence; but a heavier, direr woe for her "by whom the offence cometh." Consider, therefore, my dear young lady, with a seriousness worthy of your immortal nature, and a gravity beyond your years, the bearings of this momentous question. Resolve, in the silent depths of your reflecting spirit, "I will take care of my influence!"

Transport your mind back, through departed time, some thousand years, and enter with me one of the royal castles of England. Within one of its turret chambers behold a youthful bride, the daughter of an emperor, the wife of a king. Why is she secluded here, while the old halls of the castle are resounding with the merry voices of high-born youths and noble ladies? What is her occupation? Let that antique volume of illuminated manuscripts, containing the gems of Saxon poetry, be your answer! She finds her pleasure not in the idle pastimes of an ignorant court, but in the study of polite literature. She is devoted to the duty of self-culture to the full extent of her means and opportunities. Now, as we gaze on this enthusiastic young woman, it would appear romantically improbable, if I were to predict that her influence would lead to the elevation of England from a state of semi-barbarism, obscurity and impotency, to a position so potential and commanding as to make her feared, envied and admired, by all the other nations of earth. Yet what would have then seemed romantic as a prediction, is now an historical fact. For this lady's name is JUDITH, the stepmother of that great prince, ALFRED, whose talents and genius laid the foundations of England's legal, commercial and intellectual superiority. And it was to Judith he was indebted for the first awakening of his intellectual life, the development of his noble qualities, and the formation of his splendid character. Hence, but for the influence of this superior princess, Alfred would never have been what he was; and his country would never, perhaps, have achieved the stupendous greatness which it now possesses, by which it does, and will, perhaps to the end of time, affect the destinies of the world.

The design of this illustration is to remove from your mind that incredulity which arose in it as you read my remarks concerning the immense extent and duration of individual influence. You thought it impossible that you, a young lady, could possess such a fearful power for good or ill. Had the youthful Judith been told the precise results of her influence on the world, she would have ridiculed the statement, and have pronounced its author insane. Yet there stands its living record, in the history and condition of the British nation. And, since a corresponding power resides in your soul, who can imagine the fathomless depths of the consequences which are yet to proceed from its exercise? Your sex, instead of shielding you from the necessity of exerting such power, exposes you to it in the strongest manner; for it brings you in contact with mind when in its most impressible state, and when your influence over it is abounding, and almost absolute. You think, perhaps, if you were of the other sex, and your sphere was with warriors, statesmen and magistrates, on the public arena of life, there might be at least a possibility of your casting a stone into the sea of humanity, whose ever enlarging influence would be seen circling immeasurably far into the misty future. But your sphere is private, limited and feminine, and cannot afford scope for such results, you think. Vain thought! You are a sister, and may mould a brother's mind to virtue and to usefulness. You are a daughter, and for your sake your father may put forth efforts of unbounded might. You may hereafter bear the honored name of wife, and the more sacred one of mother. Your influence may then determine the character of your husband, and fix the destiny of your children. It may make your son an Augustine, a Washington, an Oberlin, a Wesley; or it may leave him to curse his race, with pestiferous teachings, like Socinus or Murray, with wars of ambition, like Napoleon, or with a baleful legacy of infidelity and vice, like Hume or Carlyle. For who can imagine that if Monica had been an irreligious woman, Augustine would have been a holy bishop? If Washington's mother had not inspired him with the principles of self-denying patriotism, his country might have found him a tyrant, instead of a father. And but for the sterling qualities found in the mothers of Oberlin and Wesley, the name of the former would never have adorned the annals of benevolence with such enchanting beauty; nor would the latter have erected that vast ecclesiastical fabric, whose strong and rapid growth is the greatest moral wonder of the last century. Say not, therefore, that because you are a woman your influence must be limited, but remember that your sex places you at the head-waters of the great river of humanity, where a pebble may change the direction of the streamlet.

It is said that a little boy in Holland was returning one night from a village, to which he had been sent by his father on an errand, when he observed the water trickling through a narrow opening in the dyke. He paused, reflected on the consequences that might follow if that aperture was not closed. He knew, for he had often heard his father relate the sad disasters proceeding from such small beginnings, that in a few hours that opening would enlarge, and let in the mighty mass of waters pressing on the dyke, until, the whole defence being washed away, the adjacent village would be destroyed. Should he hasten home and alarm the villagers, it would be dark before they could arrive, and the orifice might, even then, be so large as to defy attempts to close it. Prompted by these thoughts, he seated himself on the bank of the canal, stopped the opening with his hand, and patiently awaited the approach of some villager. But no one came. Hour after hour rolled slowly past in cold and darkness, yet there sat the heroic boy, shivering, wet and weary, but stoutly pressing his hand against the dangerous breach. At last the morning broke. A clergyman, walking up the canal, heard a groan and sought for its author. "Why are you here, my child?" he asked, surprised at the boy's position.

"I am keeping back the water, sir, and saving the village from being drowned," responded the child, with lips so benumbed with cold they could scarcely articulate the words.

The astonished minister relieved the boy. The dyke was closed, and the danger which had threatened hundreds of lives averted. "Heroic boy! what a noble spirit of self-devotedness he displayed!" you exclaim. True; but what was it that sustained him in his mission through that lonesome night? Why, when his lips chattered, his limbs trembled and his heart palpitated, did he not fly to the warmth and safety of home? What thought bound him to his seat? Was it not the responsibility of his position? Did he not restrain every desire to leave it, by the thought of what would follow, if he should? His mind pictured the quiet homes and beautiful farms of the people inundated by the flood of waters, and he determined to maintain his position or to die.

And ought not the higher and more weighty responsibility of your position — possessing, as you do, the power to turn a tide of endless death, or a stream of perennial life, upon the pathway of mankind — to beget in you a purpose, stern, resolute, inflexible, to be true to your position, and to use your influence for good, and not for evil? Say not of yourself, in careless, self-abandonment to circumstances,

"I am as a weed
Flung from the rock, on ocean's foam to sail
Where'er the surge may sweep, the tempest's breath prevail."

But take your stand before the world, with an invincible determination — with

"An earnest purpose for a generous end."

Consecrate your influence to virtue, to humanity, to God. Thus, in your life, you shall be "like a star glittering in its own mild lustre, undimmed by the radiance of another, and uneclipsed by the deep shades of the midnight heavens."

In that remarkable work, entitled the "Connection of the Physical Sciences," by MARY SOMERVILLE 1 find this interesting example of the cohesive power by which the atoms of material substances are held together. The manufacturers of plate glass, after polishing the large plates of which mirrors are to be made, carefully wipe them and lay them on their edges, with their surfaces resting on one another. It not unfrequently happens, that, in a short time, the cohesion is so powerful they cannot be separated without breaking. Instances have occurred where two or three have been so perfectly united, that they have been cut and their edges polished, as if they had been fused together; and so great was the force required to make their surfaces slide, that one tore off a portion of the surface of the other!

How mighty must be that force, which, acting on these plates, binds them in inseparable unity! The same cohesion unites the particles of our globe, and is the force that prevents it from crumbling into atoms. But, mighty as it is, it is invisible. How it acts, no mind has yet discovered. We see its effects, but we cannot perceive its operations. Yet who is so foolhardy as to deny its existence, because it refuses to reveal its presence, or unfold the mystery of its action? Nay, we concede it as a fact demonstrated by every material substance that meets our eyes.

By similar evidence — that of facts — we are compelled to admit that powerful influences are exerted by one mind upon another. These facts are overwhelming, both in number and in weight. Yet who can perceive the transmission of influence? Often, when we are utterly unconscious of what we do, others are receiving indelible impressions from our words, looks or actions, — impressions which will affect their destiny, and that of the world, forever. We forget this, and act without respect to others, in a great degree, because we do not see the power we exert. A young lady, who would shrink appalled at the idea of daily puncturing her brother's eye with a needle, to the destruction of his sight, will breathe a spirit of discontent, pride and folly, into his mind; and thus, by disturbing his happiness at home drive him to seek congenial society abroad, where his morals grow depraved, his character is lost, and his soul ruined. This fearful result she brings about, without a sigh of regret or a pang of sorrow. When the evil work is done, she weeps over the wreck, and would give the gold of the world to restore the fallen one. Yet for her share in causing this destruction she sheds not a tear; indeed, she is unconscious that any portion of the blame lies at her door. Her influence was silent and invisible when in exercise, and yet it drove her brother to ruin.

Another peculiarity of influence is the distance of the effect from the cause. Years will often elapse between the sowing of the seed and the ripening of the fruit — between the uttered thought, the angry glance, or the decisive act, and its result. LONGFELLOW has a beautiful illustration of this, in one of his poems. He bids you stand on the bright greensward! Shoot an arrow into the air! You watch its upward flight, as it cleaves the sky; but its fall is so swift that your eye fails to detect its resting-place. You search in vain to find it, and pronounce it lost. Long, long afterward, while wandering over the field, you perceive the lost shaft entire, sticking in an aged oak!

Again: you breathe a sweet song into the air. It falls, you know not, think not, where; but long, long afterwards, you may find it in the heart of a friend! It is thus with influence, for good or evil. Its consequences are often hidden from the eye for many years. Many of them — perhaps the most — will remain thus secret until the day which will discover to a universe the things that were done in public or in private life.

Picture to your mind a young mother, with her little boy scarce seven years old. She lifts him from his couch in the morning, and with mild words bids him kneel and say his infant prayers. Obediently he drops upon his knees. With upraised hands, closed eyes, and gentle voice, he sends up his oft-repeated petition. Presently he is silent. Then, with her hands softly resting upon his head, a voice of touching melody, and a heart overflowing with true maternal love, she breathes a holy prayer for her child. Sweet is the air of that chamber; delightful the emotions of that little bosom; and pure is the love with which he embraces his devoted mother, when their matin prayers are ended. At the vesper hour this scene is repeated; and thus, day by day, this pious woman strives to bring down holy influences upon her child's heart. Before her boy has well passed his seventh year, however, she is called by the angel of death to the spirit land, little dreaming of the immense power and duration of her influence, hereafter to be exercised over the world through that boy. Yet, in after years, her pure image haunted his memory, rebuking his vices and beckoning him to the ways of virtue and religion, until he kneeled at the cross of Christ. He became an eloquent and successful minister, an author and a sacred poet. Through his labors, CLAUDIUS BUCHANAN, one of the apostles of missionary effort in India, and the instrument of awakening the attention of that great Burmese missionary, JUDSON, to the wants of India, was converted. Through him, also, SCOTT, the commentator, was led to Christ, and to the consequent production of his valuable commentary. Another of his converts was WILBERFORCE, the champion of African freedom, and the author of that

"*Practical View of Christianity,*" which, among other great results, brought LEGH RICHMOND into the ranks of Christian discipleship, and inspired him with that heavenly spirit which fitted him to write that most useful of tracts, "*The Dairyman's Daughter.*" That boy was the Rev. JOHN NEWTON, and that woman was his mother. How immeasurable was the influence she exerted in that solitary chamber, so silently, and through the heart of a child! Yet it was long before it began to yield its fruit. For nearly twenty years it was apparently dead in his heart; but it sprung forth at last, and was, as we have shown, superabundantly fruitful.

An example of evil influence, working through centuries of time, and upheaving like a volcano, long after its author slept in death, is found in the case of LOUISA OF SAVOY, the mother of Francis the First, King of France. She lived when the Reformation began to unfold its energies on the soil of France. For a moment it commanded her attention; it seized on her convictions, but obtained no hold upon her depraved affections. The Princess MARGARET, her daughter with other noble ladies, the aristocratic Bishop of Meaux, and several eminent scholars, embraced it with fervor, and labored for it with zeal. It needed only the friendship of LOUISA to secure its triumph. For a time she permitted it to spread unchecked; but when her son Francis had endangered the stability of his throne, and lay a prisoner of war in Spain, political considerations decided this dissolute queen-mother to assume an attitude of persecuting hostility towards it. She invoked the spirit of persecution, set the unhallowed machinery of the inquisition in motion, and thus began that terrible process of cruelty, which, after centuries of conflict and bloodshed, succeeded in extirpating it from the soil. Sad have been the consequences to France. The Reformation expelled, infidelity sprung up, rank and poisonous; it became the animating spirit of the people, until, mad with its excitement, they waded through pools of blood to the altar of reason, and daringly defied the God of heaven. It is by no means difficult to see the connection between the anarchical proceedings of modern France and the conduct of Louisa of Savoy. It was in her power to confirm and establish the Reformation, and thus give blessing, honor and prosperity, to her country: she chose to persecute it. Her spirit was transmitted to posterity, and lives, in its most baleful effects, at the present hour. How truly has influence been compared to the bubbling spring, which dances up from a little crevice in a mountain recess, and sends forth a tinkling stream, so small that a "single ox, on a summer's day, could drink it dry." Yet it speeds unnoticed on its way, levying contributions upon its sister springs, and mingling with other streams, until it acquires force sufficient to cut itself a broad, deep pathway between the hills; and lo! hundreds of miles from its source, it flows in imposing magnificence, bearing proud navies on its ample bosom, until, with resistless impetuosity, it rushes into the vast waters of the "boundless sea."

I fancy—perhaps I am mistaken—that your mind refuses to feel the full impression concerning the importance of individual influence which the facts herein described are calculated to produce, because of the comparative obscurity of your sphere. You say to yourself, "Were I a princess or a queen, I might, like Judith or Louisa, set in motion immutable, potent and immortal influences; but I move in a narrower sphere, and such things are impossible for me."

Reason not thus, young lady, I pray you, lest you throw off a sense of responsibility that it were better to retain. It is *influence* that is thus powerful, not the influence of those in high stations. The effect of their conduct is more easily traced, because it works through public affairs. But the influence of a beggar girl is as potential in her sphere as is that of a queen in her more enlarged circle. Wealth, station, talent, may add to the force and extent of influence, but they cannot create it. It is an attribute of your nature, inseparable from it, inherent in it Obscurity cannot prevent its exercise. The possible consequences of your actions upon others are as measureless as those that proceed from the acts of that puissant lady, Queen VICTORIA. They *may* be equally, nay, transcendently more precious, even though you are a lonely orphan girl, dependent upon others for your support. That timely word of affectionate interest for her lord, dropped by the Syrian damsel in the ear of her mistress, is an example. It brought health to a great warrior, — it led him to a knowledge of the true God; to the spread of the Divine name; and it has lived through centuries, stimulating untold thousands to speak words of love and to do deeds of benevolence. Obscurity has no power, therefore, to neutralize this gift. If you exist, you must exert power over others, for weal or woe.

At the close of a summer's day, a group of laughing girls sat on the steps of a pavilion which stood, a summer residence, in the midst of beautiful grounds. The air rung with their merry voices, and the groves echoed back their laughter. "What," said one of them, "should we choose for our lot, if some good fairy should stand before us, and grant us each a wish?"

"I would choose to be a countess, with my hawks and hounds to hunt withal," cried one, her dark eye gleaming with the pride which inspired the wish.

"I would found a college," said another, whose ample brow and intelligent features proclaimed her own love of literature.

"I would build a hospital that should be a house of refuge for the poor, and a home for the sick, — where love might soothe their pains and lighten their burden of sorrow," replied a third, while a tear of benevolence, sparkling in her eye, declared the tenderness of the heart that prompted this wish.

"And if I were married, I would — "

A loud laugh interrupted this fourth speaker. It came from the father of the girls, who, unperceived, had approached the party, and overheard their wishes. After some exclamations of surprise had died away, the father, who was no less a personage than the famous Sir THOMAS MORE, announced his purpose to grant the wish of his daughter Mercy, and build a hospital. The hospital was erected, and many a disconsolate heart found shelter and comfort within its walls. So potent was that wish, idly uttered in a moment of girlish gayety.

The lesson inscribed on this fact is the uncertainty which attaches to the particular acts of life It shows a careless word prolific of highly beneficial results, bringing joy to many hearts. In like manner, a careless word may do evil. Hence, we never know the real importance of our own acts. We cannot judge which of them will be most influential. A truth that invests every detail of life with moral grandeur, and demands the liveliest attention to our minutest actions.

Permit me, young lady, to ask you how you are to wield this tremendous element of power, with benefit to others, unless you do it by the aid of Divine grace? How can you consecrate it to goodness, unless the Almighty Spirit of goodness imparts the power? How can you attain the wise thoughtfulness, the lofty aim, the unselfish motive, the resolute will, so essential to right influence, unless from the indwelling of the Holy Spirit of love, wisdom and purity? How can you, so weak, so thoughtless, so inexperienced, safely guard and rightly expend, this priceless treasure, in your own unassisted strength? It is impossible! You could as easily create an archangel with a word, as to rightly exert your influence without the religion of Jesus Christ. Reject him, and retributive justice will write anathema on your influence. You shall feed on its terrible fruit forever. As a spectre, with your name written in distortion on its face, it shall stand before you. It shall draw the curtain of your couch when you sleep, and extend you an ice-cold hand. It will stand before you at the hour of death, and thrust aside your last prayer. It will stand upon your grave in the resurrection, and at your side when God shall judge you.* But, by embracing Christ, the will, the motive, the power to consecrate your influence to beneficent ends, will be given you. You will move as an angel of goodness on earth. Your influence, living after your death, will remain

> "A rill, a river, and a boundless sea,"

upon whose waters numberless trophies shall be borne, to adorn your triumph when you take your place among the victors in the kingdom of God.

* See Schiller.

CHAPTER IV.

THE TRUE SPHERE OF WOMAN.

THE heroic achievements of the shepherdess of Domremi, JOAN OF ARC, are no doubt familiar to my young reader. Her imaginary inspiration; her enthusiastic persistence in the execution of her supposed mission; her daring courage, as, armed cap-a-pie and mounted on a fiery warhorse, she led the embattled hosts of France to victory; her success, her sincerity, her melancholy fate,—have awakened your wonder, your admiration, and your pity. Her romantic elevation from the peasant's hut to the palaces of kings, her brilliant but brief career, her astounding influence over proud ecclesiastics, haughty nobles and great princes, her unquestionable and successful patriotism, are written indelibly upon your imagination. But I am bold to presume that, with all your surprise at her deeds, you have never really *loved* her character Not that there is nothing lovely in it; but her masculine attitude casts so deep a shadow upon her more womanly qualities, you feel constrained to withhold your love. You cannot sympathize with a woman warrior. Her position, as a military leader and combatant, unsexes her before your feelings, and you rank her with the anomalies of your sex.

On the contrary, you can contemplate the character of HANNAH MORE with a truly affectionate regard — albeit she too was a patriotic defender and savior of her nation. You can contemplate her amiable spirit, heaving with anxious concern at the dangers which hung over her country, at a period when revolution and anarchy threatened its institutions. You can study her mind laboring to discern a method by which she could aid in warding off the impending danger. You can witness her studious labors with the pen, and read her earnest appeals to the loyalty and good sense of the English people, through her popular tracts. You can trace the success of these appeals in the altered feelings of thousands toward the government, and in the constitutional and peaceful reforms subsequently brought to pass in that country. You can hear her named, by the voice of Fame, as having been one of the principal instruments of saving the nation, — but no repugnant feeling rises in your breast toward her. You can admire her talents, her patriotism, wonder at her success, and, withal, you can ardently love her character. While Joan of Arc lives in your *imagination*, Hannah More occupies a place in your *affections*.

For this difference in your feelings, you are not responsible. Your repugnance to the character of Joan of Arc, and your affectionate regard for that of Miss More, are alike instinctive. They both flow from the constitution of your nature. They are not peculiar to your own mind, nor to your own sex. There are few, if any, minds uninfluenced by peculiar opinions, that would not be similarly affected, at once, by an impartial view of these two characters

The same remarks are applicable to all other women of corresponding qualities. Who, for example, can love the masculine energy of that really strong-minded woman, Queen ELIZABETH? Her qualities, great and high as they were, cannot command our affections, even though she stands before us as the "good Queen Bess." So with MARTHA GLAR, the Swiss heroine, who led over two hundred women to the field of Frauenbrun and to death, in defence of liberty; with JAEL, the destroyer of Sisera; and with every other woman who has stepped over the sphere which nature, with unerring wisdom, has assigned to her sex. While VOLUMNIA and VIRGILIA, the mother and wife of Coriolanus, who saved their country by affectionate appeals to the love and patriotism of that indignant warrior,—Lady JANE GREY, who chose imprisonment and death rather than to shed English blood in defence of her claims,—and even Queen VICTORIA, in whom the woman is more prominent than the queen, with hosts of others, who have blended true womanly qualities with great and heroic deeds, live in the affections of both sexes. How clear, therefore, is the truth, that women in their proper sphere can manifest noble qualities, and be appreciated; but women out of their sphere, while their deeds may command partial admiration, cannot be beloved or appreciated like the former. And this is not the result of conventional habits or opinions. It is a law of the human mind, from which there can be no successful appeal. If nature designed men and women to move in one and the same sphere, this intuitive repugnance toward masculine ladies would be unknown. They would rather be hailed with acclamation and viewed with pleasure, as models for their sex.

I should not have intruded the question of woman's sphere upon your attention, young lady, but for the claims so notoriously set up by a certain class of modern agitators in favor of what is technically called "woman's rights." These invaders of ancient ideas, who appear to regard everything as error which has the sanction of antiquity, and everything as truth which is novel, would lead you on a vain crusade, for political, governmental and ecclesiastical parity, with the other sex. The ballot-box, the hustings the bar, the halls of legislation, the offices of state, the pulpit, are demanded as fitting arenas for the exercise of your talents. There ought to be no barrier in your way to any position in society whatever, merely because you are a woman. And you are wronged, injured and proscribed, so long as you are debarred, either by law or prejudice, from entering any sphere you may prefer. Such are the claims set up and advocated for your sex, by those who would have you not a woman, but an Amazon.

Against these views I know that your woman's nature utters its indignant protest, which is endorsed with equal emphasis by your physical constitution. And the voice of that sacred charter of woman's rights, — her great emancipator, — the Gospel of Jesus Christ, supports this protest of your nature, and rebukes the audacity of these modern innovators. The Saviour, while he invited woman to listen to his voice, permitted her to minister to his comfort, and to hover, like an angel of love, about his path of sorrow, never called her to his side as an apostle, nor sent her forth as a public teacher of mankind. His truth, entering her gentle spirit, added lustre to her virtues, and consecrated her skill to deeds of mercy. It produced a MARY, with her meek loveliness; a DORCAS, with her benevolent care for the poor; a LYDIA and an "ELECT LADY," with their noble hospitality. It made delicate and trembling girls heroic martyrs; but it never produced a bold declaimer, an Amazonian disputant, nor a shameless contender for political and ecclesiastical rights. It elevated her, but left her in her own sphere. It increased her influence, but it never changed her mission. Neither does the Gospel intimate that at the climax of its triumph it will remove her from her distinct and appropriate sphere.

Permit me, by way of illustrating another feature of this question, to lead you into the sitting-room of a respectable and pious lady. She is neatly but plainly attired, and is busy, with the aid of a servant, dusting and cleaning the room. The door-bell rings, and the girl hastens to see who is the visitor. She finds the lady's pastor at the door, and, without ceremony, ushers him into the sitting-room. The lady's face is suffused with blushes, as she confusedly lays aside her dusting-brush, and offers her hand to the minister, saying, "Sir, I am ashamed you should find me thus."

"Let Christ, when he cometh, find me so doing," replies her pastor.

"What, sir! do you wish to be found in this employment?" earnestly inquires the astonished lady.

"Yes, madam, I wish to be found faithfully performing the duties of my mission, as I have found you fulfilling yours."

And was not the minister right? He recognized a great, but a despised truth. He saw as high a moral importance in the humble task of the lady as in the missions of Gabriel to the ancient prophets: for both did the will of God in their respective spheres; and diversity of sphere does not necessarily involve real inferiority in the employment. The lady in her home could exhibit an affection as true, and an obedience as sincere, as the angel in his sphere. It would be difficult to show wherein her employment was morally and necessarily inferior to his, inasmuch as the character of an act derives all its moral greatness, not from the sphere of the actor, but from its conformity to the will of God.

Do you perceive the bearing of my illustration upon the question of woman's sphere? It shows you that your sex is not necessarily inferior to the other, because it is called, by God and nature, to act in a different sphere. Your exclusion from the stage of public life does not imply your inferiority,—only the *diversity* of your powers, functions and duties. Indeed, it would defy the loftiest powers to show wherein the work, the mission or the sphere of woman, is a whit beneath that of her more bustling and prominent companion — man.

What is the sphere of woman? Home. The social circle. What is her mission? To mould character, — to fashion herself and others after the model character of Christ. What are her chief instruments for the accomplishment of her great work? The affections. Love is the wand by which she is to work moral transformations within her fairy circle. Gentleness, sweetness, loveliness and purity, are the elements of her power. Her place is not on life's great battle-fields. Man belongs there. It is for him to go forth armed for its conflicts and struggles, to do fierce battle with the hosts of evils that throng our earth and trample upon its blessings. But woman must abide in the peaceful sanctuaries of home, and walk in the noiseless vales of private life. There she must dwell, beside the secret springs of public virtue. There she must smile upon the father, the brother, the husband, when, returning like warriors from the fight, exhausted and covered with the dust of strife, they need to be refreshed by sweet waters drawn "from affection's spring," and cheered to renewed struggles by the music of her voice. There she must rear the Christian patriot and statesman, the self-denying philanthropist and the obedient citizen. There, in a word, she must form the character of the world, and determine the destiny of her race. How awful is her mission! What dread responsibility attaches to her work! Surely she is not degraded by filling such a sphere. Nor would she be elevated, if, forsaking it, she should go forth into the highways of society, and jostle with her brothers for the offices and honors of public life. Fame she might occasionally gain, but it would be at the price of her womanly influence.

Fancy yourself far out at sea, in a noble ship, contending with a furious storm. A "war of mountains" rages on the surface of the great deep;—they seem "to swallow each other," and to "reproduce new Alps and Andes from their monstrous depths," to keep up the strife.

> "Beneath is one wild whirl of foaming surges;
> Above, the array of lightnings, like the swords
> Of Cherubim, wide brandished, to repel
> Aggression from heaven's gates."

Behold, amidst this scene of grandeur, the stormy petrel gliding up the face of a huge wave, darting above the foam of a breaker, or sweeping along the watery valleys, as composedly and as naturally as it ever swept over the same sea in an hour of calm. Behold, too, another bird, whirling and darting above the spray, with a cry of seeming despair; now flying before a monster sea, and anon struggling to keep its wet and weary wings from folding into helpless inaction. But see! it descries your ship, and, prompted by an instinct of self-preservation, flies toward it for shelter. Alighting, it hides under the lee of your bulwarks, in a coil of cable. Mark its exhaustion! See how its wet breast heaves with the violent beating of its little heart! Its fright is excessive, and it is questionable if it will recover itself or live.

Tell me, lady, why this little trembler is in so pitiful a plight, while the stormy petrel gambols freely among the waves! You cannot answer. Then listen! The petrel is in its appropriate sphere. The little trembler is a land-bird, tempted, at first, by sunny weather, to wander among the islands, and driven, at last, by a strong wind to sea. He is out of his sphere; and hence his quiet has fled, his song is silenced and his life endangered. God made him for the land; the grove is his home, and his sphere is among the flowers.

It is thus with the entire creation. Everything has its appointed sphere, within which alone it can flourish. Men and women have theirs. They are not exceptions to this truth, but examples of it. To be happy and prosperous, they must abide in them. Man is fitted for the storms of public life, and, like the petrel, can be happy amidst their rudest surges. Woman is formed for the calm of home. She may venture, like the land-bird, to invade the sphere of man, but she will encounter storms which she is utterly unfitted to meet; happiness will forsake her breast, her own sex will despise her, men will be unable to love her, and when she dies she will fill an unhonored grave.

That great patriot, JOHN ADAMS, paid a high compliment to the power of your sex, when, in an hour of deep political gloom, he wrote the following lines to his wife. Alluding to the attack of the British on the city of Philadelphia, he says: "I believe the two Howes have not very great women for their wives; if they had, we should suffer more from their exertions than we do. A smart wife would have put Howe in possession of Philadelphia a long time ago."

This remark of the statesman, playfully as it is expressed, was, nevertheless, the offspring of an opinion which he seriously maintained concerning the influence of women. He contended that much of the merit of the great men, whose names are on the roll of fame, belonged to their sisters, wives and mothers. Hence he attributed the faults of Howe to the lack of high merit in his wife.

JOHN QUINCY ADAMS, the "old man eloquent," once paid the following precious tribute to his mother. "It is due to gratitude and nature, that I should acknowledge and avow that, such as I have been, whatever it was, such as I am, whatever it is, and such as I hope to be in all futurity, must be ascribed, under Providence, to the precepts and example of my mother."

Very similar is the confession of the celebrated German philosopher, KANT, who says, "I shall never forget that it was my mother who caused the good which is in my soul to fructify."

It was to his devoted sister that the pious PASCAL was indebted for preservation from a worldly spirit.

which at one time threatened to drag him down from the heights of a holy experience to the depths of sin. But for her, his light might have been quenched forever.

The martyr missionary, MARTYN, was also led to Christ by the gentle hand of his sister, who thus called into action those mighty energies in his soul which made his life an example of self-denying labor.

I quote these honorable acknowledgments from these great minds to confirm the opinion of John Adams, and to impress it forcibly upon your heart. You must consider them as specimen facts. Could every great and good man arise from the dead, to make known from whence the power came which called his noblest qualities into action, each would point to a sister, wife or mother. What can ambition in a woman's heart ask more? What if she is forbidden to stand in the forum, to mount the rostrum, to enact the part of a Cicero, a Washington, a Wesley? Has she therefore nothing great in her destiny? Is it nothing to sit beside young, unformed intellect, and, by the skilful strokes of her chisel, give it such shape and beauty as shall command the admiration of a world? Is that gift to be despised which enables a woman, with almost unerring certainty, to determine the character of her brother, husband or son? Nay! She who trains a soul to right and noble deeds "stands higher in the scale of benefactors than he who unshackles a continent from thraldom; for she adds more to the sum of human happiness, if we estimate the effects by their duration." *

Nor are the pleasures of success less delightful in a woman's breast, because she attains it through another. If a rich tide of joy flows through the breast of an applauded hero, a triumphant statesman or a useful philanthropist, there is another equally delightful in the bosom of the woman who is conscious that, but for her, the great man would never have mounted the pedestal of his greatness.

Behold, for an example, a splendid scene enacted at the close of the Revolutionary war. CORNWALLIS

* See Chalmers' Memoirs, vol. I., p. 246.

and his army had been captured. The Revolution was successful. The great chiefs and officers of the victorious armies were assembled at a festival in honor of their victory. The spacious saloon was crowded. There were those chivalrous Frenchmen, in their gorgeous uniforms, who, at the cry of liberty, had bravely rushed to arms, and whose valor had been proved in many a hard-fought field. There were those sturdy continentals, whose daring courage and unconquerable spirit had triumphed over the disciplined bravery of their English opponents. There, also, were the women, the matrons of that heroic age, with their blushing daughters, all radiant with the sunny spirit of joy which reigned throughout that brilliant assembly.

Presently the doors of the saloon open to admit a personage, whose entrance awakens universal attention. His figure is noble and commanding; his bearing dignified, without haughtiness; his expression lofty, but mild. He treads the floor with unaffected, yet unsurpassed majesty. His presence kindles every eye and heart with the ardor of rapturous enthusiasm.

He is regarded with reverence, yet with affection, — as a superior, and yet as a friend. He presents to their gaze the rare sight of a Christian soldier and an unambitious statesman. He combines in himself the daring of a Cæsar with the caution of a Fabius, — the patriotism of a Regulus and the virtue of a Cincinnatus. He is the man whose enduring fortitude, military prowess, and overawing influence, had sustained the spirit of the Revolution, crowned it with success, and earned for himself the glorious preëminence of being the "first in war, first in peace, and first in the hearts of his countrymen," — for that personage was George Washington!

Never, perhaps, was homage more sincerely or heartily rendered to a man than by the brave and beautiful in that hall; and never was it more deserved. Nor is it possible to conceive of a purer, sweeter human joy, than that which swelled his bosom.

There was another heart, however, that shared in the homage and the joy of that occasion. Leaning on the arm of the hero, in simple stateliness of mien, there walked MARY, THE MOTHER OF WASHINGTON She had trained him in his boyhood, — taught him the principles and developed the qualities which lay at the foundation of his greatness. It was her hands which had moulded his character to symmetry and moral beauty. Her prayers, her influence, and her instructions, had repressed and restrained the growth of evil qualities, and cultivated that divine life in his soul, which led him to take counsel of the God of battles — the Governor of nations. Her early influence over her glorious son was well understood, and silently acknowledged, in that gay assembly. Yea, her son had owned it, — was proud of it. He laid his lofty honors at her feet, and prized her smile above the noisy voices of fame. Did she then experience a pleasure aught inferior to his? Who shall decide which bosom was the happiest on that triumphant day? The joy of Washington was great; the joy of his mother was, at least, equal. Would she have accomplished more, or tasted a sweeter pleasure, if, forsaking her sphere, she had mingled directly in the councils of the states and the movements of the camp? Impossible! She helped to achieve the Revolution, — she shared the richest enjoyments of its success; but she did it through her heroic son, — just as God would have every woman win her honors and rewards, through her brother, husband or child.

Away, then, from your heart, young lady, with all the vagaries of these pseudo reformers! Treat their crude opinions with the contempt they deserve. Glory in the true greatness and real sublimity of the sphere you are called to fill. Labor to qualify yourself to fulfil your mission with distinguished success. Obtain, by persevering self-culture, those high qualities which lift one mind above another. For you must not fail to remember, that you cannot communicate high qualities and noble sentiments to other minds, unless they first exist in your own. Cultivate, therefore, the loftiest virtues, the highest elements of great character. Let them be chastened in yourself by that sweet sunniness of spirit, and that affectionate gentleness, which command the avenues of the human heart. Thus will you secure both respect and love. You will impress your image on some precious masculine mind in whom it shall go forth upon the great theatre of life, to act with blessing and power upon future generations.

Such being your sphere, with its weighty responsibility, you require the aids of religion to fill it with propriety and effect. High qualities are not the offspring of an ungracious nature. There is too much of the moral weakness of depravity in the human soul, to permit its harmonious and useful development, without the restraints and aids of grace. Where the spirit of revealed religion does not reign there will be moral deformity. Selfishness with its forbidding aspect, pride, envy, h[illegible] discontent, fretfulness, ill-temper, and troops of kindred vices, will wound and sear your character, diminish your influence, and disturb your peace. But, by surrendering yourself to the claims and influences of the Saviour, your life will be as a fruitful branch in a beautiful vine. The fruits of the Spirit will adorn it. Clusters of graces, such as love, joy, peace, gentleness, goodness and meekness, will give it attractiveness.

Its beauty will impress the minds around you, and act as a mighty restraint from sin upon them, as they wander over the earth. Your image will stand before a brother, a husband or a father, as a good genius in his hour of temptation, and forbid the triumph of the tempter. For, calling up your character, his full heart will exclaim of you,

> "She looks as whole as some serene
> Creation minted in the golden moods
> Of sovereign artists ; not a thought, a touch,
> But pure as lines of green that streak the white
> Of the first snow-drop's inner leaves."

To impress such an image of yourself upon some loved mind within your circle, is worth a lifetime of effort. And you have no effectual means of accomplishing so noble a task, but by communing deeply with the spirit of Jesus. Resolve, therefore, to live at his footstool, and he will inspire you with every high and holy quality necessary to enable you to fulfil your earthly mission.

CHAPTER V.

LOVELINESS OF SPIRIT.

THE author of "THE NEW TIMON," describing the character of a young heroine, who won all hearts to herself, thus explains the philosophy of her influence:

"It was not mirth, for mirth she was too still;
It was not wit, wit leaves the heart more chill;
But that continuous sweetness, which, with ease,
Pleases all round it, from the wish to please.
This was the charm that Lucy's smile bestowed;
The wave's fresh ripple from deep fountains flowed;
Below, exhaustless gratitude, — above,
Woman's meek temper, childhood's ready love."

Here the poet places an abiding sweetness of spirit, a meek loveliness of temper, as the central star .n a constellation of virtues which adorn his ideal woman. The inspired writer expressed the same high estimate of a kind and loving spirit, when he drew his admirable picture of a "*virtuous woman*," whose "*price is far above rubies.*" Of her he says, "*She openeth her mouth with wisdom, and in her tongue is* THE LAW OF KINDNESS."

This loveliness of spirit is woman's sceptre and sword, for it is both the emblem and the instrument of her conquests. Her influence flows from her sensibilities, her gentleness, her tenderness. It is this which disarms prejudice, and awakens confidence and affection in all who come within her sphere; which makes her more powerful to accomplish what her will resolves than if nature had endowed her with the strength of a giant. For, while the will of a pigmy may resist, to his destruction, the commands of a Cyclops,

> "The heart *must*
> Leap kindly back to kindness."

Speaking of this power, an elegant writer says: "If there is such a native loveliness in the sex as to make a woman victorious when in the wrong, how resistless her power when she is on the side of truth!" And even the ancient bard of Erin, OSSIAN, sung the same idea, in the days of old. Describing a maiden heroine, he says: "Loveliness, with a robe of beams, clothed the maid of Lutha, the daughter of many isles."

I would not have you imagine, young lady, that loveliness of spirit alone is a source of high and abiding influence, nor that other great qualities may be dispensed with, if this one is obtained. So far is this from the truth, that this quality is dependent upon the existence of the most exalted moral excellences. Nature may have endowed you with exquisite sensibility, with a highly refined and delicate physical organization, which may give you the appearance of being lovely, and enable you to make a favorable impression, and to exert an irresistible power over the mind you aim to fascinate. But, if your heart is lacking in high-minded self-devotion, in self-control, in sincerity, in genuine meekness, your loveliness, like a coating of gold upon a counterfeit coin, will disappear before all who behold you in contact with the realities of life. Genuine loveliness is the effulgence of sublime virtue; it is a soft and mellow light, diffusing a delicious radiance over the entire character, and investing its possessor with a halo of indefinable beauty. It is the "fresh ripple from deep fountains" of inborn love. It is the gentle dew descending from the clear heaven of a pure and lofty mind — the mystic charm that "pleases all around, from the wish to please."

Permit me to lead you to what may appear an unlikely spot to learn much of the power of loveliness — to the cell of a maniac. Behold his furious ravings at our approach! Mark his wild and terrifying expression! How fearful a thing is madness! But see! Here is a beautiful child, just able to talk. She holds a rosy apple in her tiny fingers, and with timid steps is approaching the grating of the cell. Placing the apple between two bars, she addresses the maniac in the soft and musical voice of childhood, saying, "Sir, will you please to take an apple?"

He gazes at the child a moment in stupid wonder, and then retires raving to the corner of his cell. Let a day pass, in your imagination. Again the little girl comes toddling towards the cell, and repeats her offer of love. In vain, as yet, is her appeal. Another and another day passes, with the same offer and the same result. Unwearied the little one stands, an angel of love, in the madman's presence, warbling forth her offer of "Sir, will you take an apple?" The eyes of the maniac rest a moment upon those of the child; they are full of the expression of love. He is attracted. Her sweet voice renews the request, "Will you take an apple, sir?" He is fascinated. She smiles. He is subdued. He accepts the fruit, and eats it. The keeper now opens the door of his cell. The little girl takes him by the hand, leads him forth docile as a lamb, and presents us with a lovely picture of madness conquered by the persevering kindness and loveliness of a gentle girl.

From this life-painting let us turn to another equally affecting and instructive. It contains a venerable old English market, with its busy crowds of buyers and sellers. Beneath its shadow, and near one of its corners, is a humble stall, in which stands a poor woman, rough in her exterior, but very benevolent in her looks. Her mind seems divided between the care of her stall and of an idiot boy, who sits on the ground near by, swinging backwards and forwards, and singing, in a low, pathetic voice, an unmeaning strain. The poor creature is thoroughly demented. He knows nothing, and he spends all his time seated as we behold him. His mother's love is the only ray that penetrates the chambers of his darkened mind.

One day the neighbors missed this old market-woman and her idiot son from their accustomed places. Seeking her humble hovel, they found her lying dead upon her comfortless couch, with the boy seated beside the corpse, holding her cold hand in his, and mournfully singing his accustomed strain. They spoke kindly to him. He looked at them, with a tear standing in his eye, and then, clasping the dead hand with increased tenderness, resumed his unmeaning song, but in a softer and sadder key.

"Poor wretch! what shall we do with him?" inquired the visiters. As they stood gazing on the melancholy spectacle, the boy gathered the dust from the floor in his two hands, sprinkled it upon his head, and broke forth, with a wild, clear, heart-searching pathos, into his monotonous song. Thus affectingly did this idiot lad proclaim the depth of the impression made upon his spirit by the continuous kindness of his mother, years of whose life had been wearily spent in self-devoted care for her child. The loveliness of a mother's devotedness had penetrated the soul of an idiot.

I have yet another illustrative sketch, by which to impress your heart with a conviction that the power of a kind and lovely spirit is almost irresistible. The scene is from one of those sad and dreary events so plentiful in the French Revolution. Among the prisoners in the Abbey was the venerable CAZOTTE and his lovely daughter ELIZABETH.

Finding no proofs of royalism against the daughter, the revolutionary leaders sent an order for her dismissal from the prison. Her filial heart refused the gift of liberty, and, at the cost of much personal suffering, she clung to her noble father's side in prison. Her generous self-devotion, her virtuous deportment, and the entire loveliness of her spirit, wrought wonderfully on all within the prison. Even those murderous Marseillois, whose hearts were harder than the steel of their swords, acknowledged her power, and protected the person of her father for her sake. But, on the terrible second of September, 1792, after a carnage of thirty hours in the court of the Abbey, Cazotte was summoned to meet death. "Why were you imprisoned?" demanded one of these murderers.

"You will find the answer in the jailer's book!" was the old man's stern reply.

An axe was already uplifted. The blood-stained hands were outstretched to pierce his aged breast. His daughter rushed wildly through the crowd, threw herself on the old man's neck, and presenting her bosom to the swords of the assassins, exclaimed, "Strike, barbarians! You shall not get at my father until you have pierced my heart!"

The effect of this act was irresistible. The pikes were checked. The hands of the murderers were paralyzed. The mob was overawed. A voice shouted "Pardon!" "Pardon! pardon!" replied a thousand voices, and the beautiful Elizabeth, rendered doubly beautiful by her agitation, and defended by a band of Marseillois, led her father forth from that scene of blood, amidst the thunders of their applause, to liberty and home. An example of the power of self-devoted loveliness of character over the fiercest minds.

These illustrations of the power of a kind and lovely spirit are, I admit, extreme cases. I have chosen such examples in preference to others, because they best subserve my purpose. For if kindness has power over a maniac, an idiot, an assassin, it must be sufficient to subdue minds that are more accessible to influence. If love in the heart and sweetness in the manner of the gentle girl could subdue a raving maniac, — if in the market-woman it could awaken affection in an idiot's breast, — if in Elizabeth it could charm the minds and change the purpose of murderers, — surely, in your hands, it is capable of doing much with the almost infinitely more susceptible minds that move within your sphere. Possess it, and you may bind the soul of your brother, in bonds softer than velvet and stronger than gyves of brass, to religion and virtue. You may awaken the mind of your scholars to noble aspirations after excellency on earth and glory in heaven. You may sustain the spirit of your father, and save him from yielding to despair in an hour of temptation. You may mould the destiny of your husband, and breathe the air of Paradise around his tried spirit, until he shall acknowledge you to be the good genius of his existence. You may train your children, if you ever become a mother, so that, as CORNELIA found her highest honor in being the MOTHER OF THE GRACCHI, it may be the richest thought of your life that you are the mother of patriot, philanthropic and Christian children, and that through the deeds of brother, father, husband or son, your name is to be writ in the affections of posterity. Seek, therefore, and seek earnestly, after a lovely spirit! Find it, and you will be enthroned queen of the sphere in which you move.

The citizens of ancient Rome were accustomed to place the images of their great ancestors in the vestibules of their houses. These venerable busts constantly met their eyes, and reminded them of the glorious actions of the dead. They were thus prompted to imitate the heroic examples of their illustrious fathers, and to transmit a worthy name to posterity. The idea was certainly a noble one, and was, to some extent, successful. It created a pride of character, which led to noble deeds, in a long line of glorious Romans, through many ages of that gigantic commonwealth.

This fact recognizes a great truth, which has an important bearing on the subject of power over other minds. It teaches the depth and practical results of oft-repeated impressions. Those marble busts, cold and lifeless as they were, repeated their silent lessons of virtuous heroism every day. They constantly reminded the young Roman of the glory that gathers round the name of him who forms a high character, and lives for noble aims. The idea entered his heart. He mused upon it until he did reverence to the virtues of the ancients, and resolved to tread in their consecrated steps.

It is by a corresponding process that a spirit of meek loveliness in a woman achieves its ends. Its abiding presence, its constant exhibition in the thousand daily acts of her life, in the tones of her voice, and in the spiritual atmosphere which she creates around her, gradually wins the affections of the most wilful minds. It is not by one striking act of kindness she gains her influence, but from the impression which her daily deportment makes on her associates. Her presence is a beam of light, gladdening the family circle, and its members soon learn to rejoice at her presence, to feel charmed by her character. She breathes words of kindness in every ear, her eyes beam with the light of love upon all, her feet hasten to assist all. There is a noble unselfishness in her actions, a benevolent devotion to the interests and pleasure of others, which throws a spell of enchantment over them. In her the song of the poet is realized:

"Love took up the harp of life, and smote on all the chords
with might,
Smote the chord of self, that, trembling, passed in music out
of sight."

The celebrated William Wirt, in a letter to his daughter, discourses on the power of this unselfish loveliness in woman, in the following sensible manner. He says, "I want to tell you a secret. The whole world is like the miller at Mansfield; he cared for nobody, — no, not he, — because nobody cared for him. And the whole world will serve you so, if you give them the same cause. Let every one, therefore, see that you do care for them, by showing them what Sterne so happily calls 'the small sweet courtesies of life,' in which there is no parade whose voice is too still to tease, and which manifest themselves by tender and affectionate looks and little acts of attention — giving others the preference in every little enjoyment at the table, in the field, walking, sitting or standing. This is the spirit that gives your sex its sweetest charm. It constitutes the sum total of the witchcraft of woman. Let the world see that your first care is for yourself, and you will spread the solitude of the upas-tree around you, in the same way, by the emanation of a poison which kills all the juices of affection in its neighborhood. Such a girl may be admired for her understanding and accomplishments, but she will never be beloved.

"The seeds of love can never grow but under the warm and genial influence of kind feelings and affectionate manners. Vivacity goes a great way in young persons. It calls attention to her who displays it. If it then be found associated with a generous sensibility, its execution is irresistible. On the contrary, if it be found in alliance with a cold, haughty, selfish heart, it produces no other effect than an adverse one."

I remember a young lady, ANNETTE by name, who was remarkably beautiful and extremely vivacious. These qualities attracted a splendid young man, named FREDERICK, to her side. Annette seemed so cheerful, so pleasant and so agreeable, that the youth was fascinated. He became first her daily companion, and, shortly after, her accepted lover. They appeared as if nature designed them for each other; and, in the beautiful language of TENNYSON, it

> "Nor stranger seemed that hearts
> So gentle, so employed, should close in love,
> Than when two dew-drops on the petal shake
> To the same sweet air, and tremble deeper down,
> And slip at once all fragrant into one."

But, alas! the sweetness of Annette's manners was not the beaming of a lovely spirit. It was a mask worn only in the court of pleasure, and in the gala hours of love. At home, when unwatched by all but the eyes of her family, the true features of her really unlovely spirit displayed themselves in all their hatefulness. Selfish and proud, she tyrannized over her mother, and spread the infection of a wayward temper over the entire household. If she was the idol of the party, she was the affliction of her home. Alas for her betrothed! — he was in danger of finding tinsel, where he sought gold. Happily he one day made a call at an unexpected hour. The door was open, and with a justifiable familiarity he entered the parlor. A shrill voice reached his ear; it was speaking in angry tones. Could it be Annette's voice? He listened with painful attention, and heard her, whom he supposed to be the mirror of all gentleness, scolding her mother in most unfilial language, and in all the vehemence of unwomanly passion. He quietly retired, and from that hour Annette had no lover. She had deceived him, and he felt justified in shrinking from an alliance which would be sure to embitter his life.

You may pronounce this an unfortunate discovery for Annette. But would she have gained aught for herself, if, by blinding Frederick, she had become his bride? Would not that unlovely spirit have accompanied her to her bridal home? Would it not have become a grim destroyer of its peace? Revealing itself to her husband, it would have dashed his cup of bliss to the dust, and have uncovered the deception when too late for a remedy. Then his love would have turned to loathing and to scorn, and the miserable pair would have spent their lives in mutual disgust and sorrow. Annette, though she had the power to appear lovely, lacked true loveliness of *mind,* and could not create an empire of pleasure without first remedying so essential a defect. Remember, therefore, young lady, that loveliness must exist in the spirit. Outward gentleness, like odor from a flower or music from a harp, must proceed from a soul made lovely in itself.

When that iron-minded warrior, CAIUS MARIUS, was taken prisoner in the marshes of the LIRIS, his captors sent a Gallic soldier to his prison, with orders to put him to death. The captive sat in the darkest corner of his chamber. His eyes gleamed fiercely on his executioner, and in a voice of thunder he exclaimed, "Man! durst thou kill Caius Marius?"

The looks, the language, the voice, the energy of Marius, produced so powerful an impression upon the Gaul, that he threw down his sword and fled, declaring it was impossible to kill the prisoner.

Now, of ten thousand other men, probably not one in

similar circumstances would have so moved this fierce Gallic barbarian, even had he used the same words. Why, then, did Marius affect him so powerfully? There was uncommon might and power in his great spirit. He possessed extraordinary energy of mind, which, from a habit of commanding others, he had learned to throw into his words and looks. Thus his mind acted, beyond the power of the mere words he uttered, upon the mind of the soldier, and completely paralyzed his action. All minds possess this attribute of expressing their qualities through words and looks, and are constantly making impressions upon other minds thereby, according to the kind and measure of their power.

This power of the mind to act on others by spiritual impressions is one of its most surprising qualities, and perhaps, from the constancy of its operation, its chief source of influence. And as is the mind, so is the impression it makes. As the image must first be in the die before it can impress the coin, so must the impression made upon other minds exist first in the spirit of her who makes it. Hence the impossibility of simulating a lovely spirit. The manners of a lady may be polished, her air soft and graceful, and the countenance wreathed in smiles; but unless the soul itself is lovely, the impression made by the character will be unfavorable, at least, on those with whom she constantly associates. The mental habit will betray itself. If unloving and unlovely, it will display its features, in spite of the most artful precautions. If really lovely in itself, its beams will cast their lustre on the outward manners, and thereby attract other minds, as surely as the fierce mental energy of Marius conquered the spirit of the Gallic soldier.

Seek, therefore, young lady, to adorn yourself with this most charming of all ornaments. Shrink from every secret moral deformity, more than you do from physical disfigurement. Repress every inward movement of unlovely emotions. Regard envy, pride, hate, revenge, selfishness, rage and kindred passions, as serpents which must have no abode in your heart; or as poisons, which, if admitted into your mental life, will produce loathsome eruptions, disgusting deformities and deadly results Keep the chambers of your soul clean and unpolluted. But every pure emotion and generous sentiment you must sedulously cultivate and foster, with persevering care. Breathe a kindly feeling for all. Desire to impart a pleasure to all with whom you meet. Live to scatter flowers of joy in every path you tread, — to be a golden beam of soft and mellow light in every home you visit. Aim to move as a loving seraph in every circle. Thus animated by inward emotions and purposes, your outward life and actions will shine with softened lustre upon all. You will sway a sceptre of hallowed power over many hearts; and, while you "draw to yourself the love of others, as the diamond drinks up the sun's rays, only to return them in tenfold strength and beauty," you will put on charms which "no beauty of known things, nor imagination of the unknown, can aspire to emulate. You will shine in colors purer and brighter than pearl or diamond or prism can reflect. Arabian gardens, in their bloom, can exhale no such sweetness as a lovely spirit diffuses."

A faithful mother was accustomed to interrogate her children, at night, concerning the good they had tried to do during the day. One night her twin daughters were silent, yet seemed, by their manners, to wish to say somewhat. By kind solicitation from their judicious mother, they were induced to tell their little tale of love. One of them said :

" I remember nothing good: only, when one of my school-mates was happy because she had gained the head of the class, I smiled on her and ran to kiss her. And she said I was good."

Her sister then said : " A little girl who sat next to me at school had lost her baby brother; I saw that while she studied her lesson she hid her face in her book and cried. I felt sorry, and laid my face on the same book, and cried with her. Then she looked up, and was comforted, and put her arms round my neck. But I do not know why she said I had done her good."

This is a picture of beauty which appeals to the heart. I love those sweet children, though I never saw them Their young spirits appear to me as vir gin founts of unselfish sensibility With what artless simplicity they unveil their souls to our eyes! Their actions were not for effect. It was not to be beloved or praised, that the one mingled her tears, and the other her smiles, with the tears and smiles of their respective companions. No. The weeping one shed tears because she "felt sorry;" the other smiled because she felt glad at her companion's joy. This was genuine loveliness, bringing forth one of its most delightful fruits, in that pure sympathy which their conduct so finely exemplified.

Let the rare sympathy of these lovely children, also, adorn your life, young lady. It is the natural and certain growth of the sweet, unselfish spirit already urged upon you. To "*rejoice with them that rejoice, and weep with them that weep,*" is the delicious pleasure of a mind rightly disposed towards others; it is also the surest method of imparting joy. We are never so precious, in the eyes of mankind, as when we enter into their feelings. As saith SCHILLER,

"How lovely,
How sweet it is, in a fair soul, to feel
Ourselves as holy things enshrined: to know
Our happiness another cheek doth kindle,
Our trouble doth another bosom swell,
Our sorrow fill with tears another's eyes."

On the contrary, a selfish, unsympathetic nature, however it may triumph over others by superior mental power, neither imparts nor gains a pleasure. It must stand dumb forever before the question of the indomitable POSA to the Spanish PHILIP, whose towering spirit aimed to stand in isolated triumph above the rest of mankind:

"When you've sunk mankind
To be your harp-strings, who will share with you
The harmony struck from them?"

I have now described and illustrated the nature, power and necessity, of loveliness of spirit. You clearly see the nature of that charm which constitutes the "witchcraft of woman." Suffer me, in all the frankness of friendship, to say, that this essential and wonder-working quality is not natural to your sex, notwithstanding the delicacy of your physical organization and the sensibility with which you are endowed. To say that women are all kind, self-devoted, sympathetic and lovely, is to contradict experience. Pride, jealousy, discontent, envy, malice, and other baleful fruits of a sinful nature, however modified in their manifestation, are as common in women as in men. As far as they exist, they make her character unlovely, they weaken her power of attraction, they reduce her measure of influence for good. How are they to be expelled? Can it be done by self-culture — by vigorous resistance of will — by the mind itself? Without doubt, much of the outward manifestation of such qualities may be thus hindered; but their growth cannot be prevented, nor their existence terminated, by human strength alone. Job has strongly expressed human imbecility, in its conflict with these evils of the heart. Hear him.

"*If I wash myself with snow water, and make my hands never so clean, yet shalt thou plunge me in the ditch, and mine own clothes shall abhor me.*"

By this striking language, we are taught that when man has done his best to purge himself, God has but to let light shine upon his heart, to make him as morally loathsome in his own eyes, as he would be physically if he were to fall into a ditch.

SAINT PAUL also made this experiment of self-purification, with all the might of his great soul. What was the result? Behold it in his pathetic cry of despair:

"*O, wretched man that I am! who shall deliver me from the body of this death?*"

By whom, therefore, is deliverance to be won? Whose hand can break the yoke of evil passions? Whose wand can bring forth beauty in the spirit? Let the apostle answer. Hear his "Io triumphe!"

"*The law of the spirit of life in Christ Jesus* HATH MADE ME FREE!" That is, the Holy Spirit, received into the heart by faith in Christ, was the means of delivering him from his evil propensities, and of enabling him to produce those fruits of the Spirit which were the ornament of his life. Go, then, dear young lady, and imitate the holy apostle. Lay the foundations of a lovely character in a converted heart. Let the grace of the Lord Jesus create you anew in his image, which is the perfection of all loveliness. Thus will you be put in possession of genuine virtue, whose lustre, shining in all your actions, will invest your character with real glory. Living to bless others, you will yourself be blessed; oecause,

"All worldly joys are less
Than that one joy of doing kindnesses."

And when, in the dying hour, you are feeling that

"Power, will, sensation, memory, fail in turn,
Your very essence seems to pass away,
Like a thin cloud that melts across the moon,
Lost in the blue immensity of heaven."

Then those you have loved, and blessed in loving them, shall watch your departing soul, and breathe after it the prayer of

"Heaven's peace upon thee, even as thou hast
Over this soul a calm of sunshine cast."

CHAPTER VI.

SELF-RELIANCE

A SWISS hunter, who supported his family, for many years, by hunting the wild chamois in the mountains around his humble chalet, was induced to give up his abode, and remove to a cottage, which stood beside a pass in the lower Alps. Here, he was often required to act as guide or host to lost or weary travellers. For these services he frequently received liberal rewards; and, for the first time in his life, became the possessor of gold. It fascinated him, and he learned to taste a strange pleasure in hoarding it up, and in listening to its chink, as he counted it unnumbered times.

It happened, on a certain day, while he was engaged in hunting, that he found a cavern in a lone mountain nook. He removed a stone which filled the entrance, that he might eat his noontide meal beneath its roof. Judge of his surprise, on entering, to perceive a vase filled with golden coins and glittering ore! The sight enchanted him. He handled the precious treasure, gazed at it, counted the coins, and was half frantic with insane joy. Nor did he stir from the spot until the day had waned. Then he securely closed the cave, for he was afraid to reveal the secret even to his wife, and returned to his cottage to dream of his magnificent discovery.

Day after day, he visited his treasure. From "early morn to dusky eve," he lay beside it, feasting his eyes upon the dazzling wealth. All his interest in his home, his wife and children, seemed extinguished. He no longer bounded over the hills in search of the wild chamois, nor cared to lend his services to the mountain traveller. His family pined for want of food. His own person grew gaunt and poor. His spirit waxed sullen and gloomy. That cave became his world. To watch the vase, and gloat upon its contents, was his life. The gold demon had enslaved him; he was dead to every other passion, save that terrible idolatry of gold.

One day, as he lay upon the ground, absorbed in counting the money, a portion of the rock that formed the cave fell from above upon his waist, and pinned him to the earth. Vainly he struggled and writhed, to escape from his strange imprisonment. Vain were his cries for aid. The cave was in a spot so wild, that even the hunters of the Alps rarely passed it in their wanderings. There, then, in fearful agony, he perished. And when, after searching vainly for a week, his friends discovered his body, the fatal gold was found firmly clutched in his dead fingers.

The folly of this foolish huntsman is so apparent, that pity for his fate is almost lost in indignation at his insane sacrifice of all the interests of life to a destructive passion. My reader shrinks from such an example, with disdainful pity. Yet many of her sex are the victims of a folly equally egregious, and no less dangerous. Possibly my reader may herself be guilty of spending these golden years of her life in devotion to the frivolous and transitory joy of the passing hour, paying no regard to those qualifications which are absolutely necessary for her subsequent conflict with real life. Her daily, hourly devotion, is paid at the shrine of some idle pleasure, which, like the hunter's gold, sways her as with the enchantment of some great magician. Amused, infatuated, thoughtless, she lives on the plenty of her paternal home, an absolute dependant upon its bounty. The future, with its thousand possibilities and probabilities of affliction, stands before her, claiming her attention and demanding preparation for its duties. It whispers her need of mental and moral qualifications, as strong foundations within her heart for self-reliance, in the day of desolation. It bids her imitate the high example of the poet, who said:

> "I from that secret store
> Wrought linked armor for my soul, before
> It might walk forth to war among mankind."

To this whisper she is deaf; or, hearing it, she turns, like GINEVRA,

> "Laughing and looking back, and flying still."

She will live in and for the present only; — for the present, which will not stay with her, but which glides past and leaves her to the mercy of that future, which, in spite of her neglect to prepare for it, will come, with its harsh realities. Will it be wonderful, if its coming should be as the falling of the stone upon the unhappy Swiss, — a cause of suffering, of ruin, of sorrow unto death? — if she should erewhile sit amid the desolations of a life-storm,

> "Like a scorched and mildewed bough,
> Leafless 'mid the blooms of May?"

I hope, therefore, young lady, you will pluck the fruit of wisdom from my illustration, and learn that one of your first duties is to acquire those qualifications which are necessary to fit you for the emergencies of life, and to enable you to rely upon yourself, if, at any time, your natural protectors should be removed by death, or forsake you through the want of affection. Young ladies whose parents are in liberal circumstances, whose wants are anticipated by loving friends, are in great danger of growing into a habit of depending wholly upon others. They insensibly learn to lean upon the arm of parental strength. They fail to acquire the power of depending upon themselves. Nay, they dare not contemplate the possibility of being compelled to do so. They transfer their sense of dependence from the father to the husband, and vainly hope that one or the other may always be at hand with the means and disposition to sustain them. They look upon themselves as on the ivy whose tendrils cling for support to the majestic oak or lofty crag; forgetting that the lightning may rend the crag or smite the oak: then, what is left to the ivy but to trail in the dust, to be

"Soiled beneath the common tread"?

Now, though dependence upon others is more natural and more fitting to woman than to man, — though, in the providence of God, she generally finds a male protector, — yet since she may be, by adverse events, thrown wholly upon her own resources, — and since, in the actual conflicts of life, with the best of parents, brothers or husbands, she will need to lean much upon herself, — I earnestly counsel you, my dear young reader, to assiduously cultivate a habit of self-reliance. Seek such attainments as will enable you to confide in yourself, — to rise equal to your exigencies. Acquire an inward principle of self-support. Then, if the rock of your early strength be smitten, and the proud oak on which you lean, with the fondness of a first affection, be blasted, you may, nevertheless, stand erect, in mournful but triumphant superiority, amid the hapless wreck.

"Hopes are fallacies. Disappointment is the only certainty of life." This is a saying you can scarcely credit. You are yet too young to readily believe that life is anything worse than a sea,

"Calm as a cradled child in dreamless slumber bound."

A few years more of life, however, will write that saying in deep lines upon your heart. You will then understand the wisdom of Napoleon's mother, Madame LETITIA, who, in the palmiest days of her son, when he was giving away crowns, dividing kingdoms, and standing on his splendid throne as the arbiter of European destiny, diligently saved her income.

"Why do you, the mother of a great emperor, so carefully labor to amass money?" asked one of her friends.

"Who knows but that one day I may have to give bread to all these kings?" was her sensible and prophetic reply. She had learned that "hopes are fallacies;" and, when the wrecks of her children's thrones lay in melancholy magnificence around her, it could hardly be said that she was disappointed.

Picture to yourself a lady in the flower of her youth, and at the height of her beauty. She is tall, and exquisitely formed. Her head is erect in natural majesty, her gait is graceful. Her features are cast in a mould of beauty. Her blue eyes, her brilliant complexion, her loveliness of expression, give a power of absolute fascination to her face. Her conversation is as charming as her countenance. Hence, she is not only the queen, but the star, of the magnificent court over which she presides. Her husband idolizes her. Her people welcome her presence with enthusiastic plaudits, that proclaim the intensity of their admiration.

Turn now to another and sadder portrait. See, standing before a legal tribunal, a woman clad in coarse rags. Her tall form is slightly bowed, yet it betrays an air of dignity. Her eyes are dim with sorrow, but at times are lighted with a few brilliant rays. Beneath the eyelids is a black circle, graved by grief and woe. Her face is pallid, and her long hair, flowing down upon her neck, is white with anguish. All eyes are turned upon her, not in love or pity, but in curiosity, in hate, or in triumph.

Do you demand the name of these ladies? Alas! both these pictures represent one celebrated woman, Marie Antoinette! In the first, she is newly arrived from Austria, and recently wedded to King Louis; in the second, she is deposed from her throne, and placed at the bar of a remorseless revolu-

tion, to receive sentence of death. A few hours after its pronouncement, her once beautiful head fell into the blood-stained basket of the guillotine, and her fair form was buried amid heaps of common dead in La Madeleine. On the register is this record: "*For the coffin of the widow Capet, seven francs.*"

Such was the descent from the pinnacle of human splendor, greatness and glory, to the profoundest deep of earthly gloom and nothingness, experienced by that once proud and haughty queen. I urge it upon you as an example of the uncertainties attached to human condition, as a warning not to place too much dependence upon those props which support your hopes, and as a reason for cultivating those qualities which lie at the basis of a reasonable and Christian self-reliance. What if fortune has a home in your father's halls, and the ease and elegances of fashionable life are at your command? What if you are the bride of a scholar, a genius, a statesman, a merchant? What if you are so surrounded by strong friends and loving hearts, that, to human eyes it seems impossible you could ever fail of either friends or external resources? What security have you for the permanency of all these friends? May not death smite your father and mother to the dust? May not adversity dissolve the fabric of your fortunes? Yea, may not some terrible passion enter the heart of your beloved, blight all his virtues, and transform him into an incarnate fiend? May you not, in consequence, find yourself friendless, helpless and unpitied? May you not thus be called upon to draw from your own inward resources? To stand alone in society, amid cold hearts and unsympathizing spirits? Ask the shade of the unfortunate Marie Antoinette for an answer. Inquire of ten thousand living daughters of misfortune, who, on life's "unsheltered walk," are like myrtle-leaves,

> "Flung to fade, to rot and die."

Yes, my young friend, you may believe me, when I affirm that all life's wealth and friendships are so fickle and fading that even the most favored young lady owes it to herself and to society to learn the art and to acquire the power of relying upon her own energies and attainments.

A consciousness of power to grapple with actual life is indispensable to a woman, in deciding the greatest question of her earthly life, — marriage. Nothing else can enable her to act independently, if she is poor, or likely to be so. Dependent poverty is one of the saddest and most tyrannical of human ills. Life is a dreary waste, its storms are heralds of certain destruction, to a helpless, friendless woman, who is conscious of an utter impotency to conquer its difficulties. There is no heart so brave as not to quail and tremble in such a hapless condition. Hear a poet, speaking of the helpless poor, under the pressure of heavy trials :

> "Their labor all their wealth ;
> Let the wheel rest from toil a single sun,
> And all the humble clock-work is undone ;
> The custom lost, the drain upon the hoard,
> The debt that sweeps the fragment from the board.
> How mark the hunger round thee and be brave, —
> Foresee thy orphan, and not fear the grave ?"

Ay, who can be brave that gazes upon an approaching evil, which she is utterly impotent to subdue? None. Hence it is that many a young lady, bereft of her parents, or anticipating such a bereavement, gives her hand, without her heart, to a husband, for the sake of a settlement. She does not love him. She is clearly aware of his unfitness to make her happy. She even shrinks, at first, with ill-concealed inward loathing, from the idea of surrendering herself to a man her heart has not chosen. She tries to summon courage sufficient to refuse him. But the consciousness of her entire inability to depend upon herself prompts the inquiry, "What shall I do? I need a home. He will at least keep me in a respectable condition in life. I must marry him." And, forthwith, she stands at the altar, and plights a love she does not feel. She becomes a wife, not from a sense of love and duty, but from the mercenary desire to obtain a shelter from the fierce storms whose violence she is unable to resist by her own powers.

How exalted and superior is the position of that

young lady, who, by a careful process of self-culture, has acquired a noble consciousness of power to sustain herself in womanly independence, should death deprive her of her natural protectors and supporters! True, she may shrink from the conflict, as the bravest soldiers may tremble in the terrible silence that precedes the hour of battle. But she makes no sacrifice to her fears. A sense of power to cope with circumstances inspires her with confidence and courage. She exhibits the firmness of MORVALE, of whom the poet sings, in his romance, that,

> "Life glowed vigorous in his deep set-eye,
> With a calm force that dared you to defy;
> And the small foot was planted on the stone,
> Firm as a gnome's upon his mountain throne."

Thus firmly she views the lonely struggle with life. She is prepared for it, and can stand self-supported amid the selfish throngs that crowd its motley stage. She is therefore at liberty to consult her heart, whenever a candidate for her hand appears. The mercenary idea is excluded. She withholds her hand, until she can give it "with her heart in it." How precious a talisman of safety, therefore, is this invaluable power of relying upon yourself!

But, laying aside the arguments already adduced, —admitting that God may vouchsafe you friends and protectors throughout the period of your mortal life, and that you are in circumstances to exclude the mercenary idea from the question of marriage,—still, self-reliance is indispensable to your happiness. As your youth changes into womanhood, whether you marry or remain single, new duties, new responsibilities, will devolve upon you, and new circumstances will grow up around you. Instead of having others to think and plan for you, you will have to think and plan for yourself. Instead of being led, you will have to lead others. You will, in many things, be thrown upon your own resources. You will be called to act new parts in society, and to meet new expectations. Should you become a wife, your husband's interests may demand the exercise of the highest attributes of character in you, to enable you to sustain, with becoming dignity, the difficulties or honors of his position. You must, then, be either as weakness and disease to his pinions, or as beauty and vigor to the wings by which he ascends to honor and fortune. And it may be that your character will determine the question of his success or defeat, in the mighty battle of life, — for many a man of high promise and golden gifts has been dragged deep into despair, by a weak-minded, inefficient wife or daughter? while, as already shown, in others, the secret springs of great achievement have been set in motion by female power. By all your hopes of a happy and prosperous life, you are bound to rely upon yourself.

There is a great fact written with the tears of woman's remorse, which, but for its immense importance, I would not name in these pages. Yet, if I forbore to do so, I might be deemed unfaithful to the task I have undertaken. Know, then, young lady, that of the thousands of your sex who have fallen from the serene heights of virtue to the deep infamy of an impure life, by far the largest number have been driven to their degradation by the iron rod of destitution. Their virtue was subdued by the fear of beggary. Trained in the lap of plenty, untaught in the art of self-dependence, they leaned upon others for support. Death or abandonment left them without guardian or protector, —

> "Like the wreck left to drift amidst the roar
> Of the great ocean with the rocky shore."

They knew not whither to fly, nor what to do for the means of subsistence. Clothed in rags, the pale and emaciated spectre of utter destitution stood before them, and filled their hearts with forebodings of a pauper's death. Then appeared the vile seducer with his eyes of fire, his smiles of deceit, his whispers of falsehood, and his promises of gold. Affrighted by poverty, and lured by insinuating voices of hypocritical pretensions, they took the fatal leap which plunged them into fathomless caverns of unutterable despair. Had they, in earlier and happier years, acquired the power of supporting themselves, and of relying upon their own mental resources, they would, in all probability have stood pure and beautiful in the ranks of virtue. Self-reliance, that strong bulwark of female virtue, would have saved them; for by it a woman defies the terrors of poverty, and maintains such an attitude of strength and dignified self-respect as keeps even the boldest tempters afar off. Her very independence of character is as an armor of proof, invulnerable to the arrows of the destroyer. Instead of attracting the eye as a suitable victim for the temples of sin, such a woman awakens only sentiments of respect and admiration; and all are ready to exclaim, as they behold her,

> "Honor to her, who, self-complete and brave,
> In strength, can carve her pathway to the grave,
> And, heeding naught what others think or say,
> Make her own heart her world upon the way."

Let me draw your attention to two queens, and to the diverse effect of their efforts, in two appalling exigencies. The one is Marie Antoinette, whose sad fall from a magnificent throne to a seven-franc coffin, in La Madeleine, I just now described. The other is Esther, once queen of the Persian Ahasuerus. The former saw her throne menaced by a terrible revolution. It hung like huge masses of black cloud over her palace; it rose formidable and furious as the dashing wave around her husband's throne. She was his idol, and had obtained irresistible ascendency over his mind. Alarmed at the danger, anxious for her husband's honor, eager to main tain the ancient monarchy, she undertook the perilous task of governing and subduing the revolution. But, alas! every step she took only increased its fury, and added to its power. Instead of appealing to the confidence of the people, and thus fanning the latent sparks of loyalty to a flame by manifestations of real regard for their interests, she contrived to appear as the personal enemy of the revolution, and thereby brought down defeat and death upon herself and family, as the reader very well knows.

Queen Esther, also, was called to behold a terrible destruction menacing herself and her entire nation. The uplifted axe, in the irresistible hand of potent despotism, gleamed horribly as it swept the air with intent to fall on the neck of a doomed nation. The dark decree for Jewish extermination, signed by the unalterable seal of Persian majesty, and committed for execution to the malicious HAMAN, seemed fated to inevitable consummation. To human wisdom there appeared no possible door of escape. Then it was that the sage MORDECAI appealed to Esther, and summoned her to the mission of saving her people. At first, her womanly spirit shrank from the trial. Roused by another appeal from Mordecai, she at length undertook the task. Most sublimely did she devote herself and crown to the heroic work. First, she consecrated her life to the national cause. Then, by fervent devotion and pure communion with her Creator, she wrought her spirit up to glorious enthusiasm. A fire like that of inspiration flashed in her dark, expressive eyes. All the majesty of high resolve, softened by the mild glow of womanly affections, irradiated her features, and made her the loveliest of "Judah's lovely daughters." Thus prepared, she entered upon her work. She appealed to the affections of her husband, and to the pride of the nation's enemy. While she inflamed the love of her lord, the king, until he panted with desire to bestow upon her the costliest proofs of his attachment, she also, with wondrous skill, drew around her foe the meshes of that net which was to entangle and destroy him. Thus holding the prey in her grasp, she seized the fitting moment, and then, with all of woman's wit and witchcraft, she converted the rushing torrent of love, that bounded through her husband's heart towards her, into a fierce tide of terrible rage against Haman. The effect was instantaneous and complete. Her foe perished, her people lived. The power that sought their death defended them. A woman's love, guided by exalted wisdom and self-sacrificing heroism, had rescued a nation from destruction.

Whence proceeded the melancholy failure of the French queen, and the complete success of Esther? Both acted in a great crisis, — both aimed at a national result, — both exerted their utmost powers. Marie failed, and perished; Esther succeeded, and lived to enjoy her triumph. That there were many and important differences in their circumstances, is admitted; and yet, it is difficult to escape the conclusion, that the strong, shrewd wisdom which saved the Jewish nation, would have gone far toward achieving a victory over the French revolution, had it been directed to that object; and that the disqualification of Marie Antoinette would have been as fatal to Mordecai and the Jews, as it was to Louis and the French monarchy. The reason of the failure of the beautiful Austrian princess is patent to all. Her youth had been misimproved. Hear the testimony of the historian ALISON. He says: "She had little education; read hardly anything but novels and romances; and had a fixed aversion, during her prosperous days, to every species of business, or serious employment."

Here is the secret of that vacillation and contradictory action which ruled in the court of Louis, at the outset of the revolution. His queen, who attempted to steer the ship of state in that tempestuous sea, was not competent to the task. She knew this, and hence dared not rely upon her own judgment. And her unfitness is to be traced to the absence of those lofty qualities of mind, which are the offspring of that early self-culture which she not only carelessly neglected, but heartily despised.

Esther, on the contrary, spent her youth in the company of Mordecai, listening to the wise counsels of his powerful and comprehensive intellect. By this means, she acquired a vigorous, reflecting and commanding mind; a consciousness of power, a confidence in herself, by which she rose equal to her duties, in a terrible crisis. Had she resembled the French queen in her youth, her illustrious name would not have stood, as it now does, at the head of the list of great, good and patriotic women.

Let Esther stimulate you, young lady, to the patient cultivation of the sources of self-reliance. Mental strength, firmness, courage, industry, perseverance, and skill, in some art or profession, lie at the foundation of this essential spirit. Seek these qualifications, and exercise them, that they may grow in you like thrifty plants. Prepare yourself for any crisis or position to which you may be called. Then, if fortunate and prosperous, your character will glow with resplendent beauty in your happy sphere. If unfortunate, and summoned to battle with adversity,

> "Your spirit, long inured to pain
> May smile at fate, in calm disdain;
> Survive its darkest hour, and rise
> In more majestic energies."

While, if you despise the wisdom which distils from these examples, — if you live in slothful, idle self-neglect during the sunny hours of youth, and trouble suddenly bursts on your defenceless head, —

> "Your mind shall sink, a blighted flower,
> Dead to the sunbeam and the shower;
> A broken gem, whose inborn light
> Is scattered, ne'er to reünite.'

CHAPTER VII.

THE SECRET SPRINGS OF SELF-RELIANCE.

DURING the crusades, a British knight, named GILBERT, was taken prisoner, and made the slave of a Saracen emir. His misfortunes excited the pity, and his manly beauty awakened the love, of the emir's daughter. By her assistance, he escaped from his ignoble bondage, and returned to England. Shortly after, the lady left her father's home, and followed him, notwithstanding she knew nothing of his address, nor of his language, except two English words, London and Gilbert. By repeating the first, she found a vessel, and reached that city. Arrived in London, she traversed the streets, crying Gilbert! Gilbert!" Curious crowds gathered round her, asking a thousand questions, none of which she understood, and to which she responded by the watchword of her love — "Gilbert!" At last, a servant of the knight recognized her, and informed his master. Admiring the strength and romantic heroism of her affection, and bound by a sense of knightly honor, the brave crusader led her to the altar, and made her his rejoicing bride. That lady afterwards became the mother of the celebrated Thomas à Becket, — a prelate, whose power was feared even by his royal master, the King of England.

Now, however we may admire the simplicity and the love of this maiden, we cannot fail to perceive her imprudence. That she was successful, does not diminish the actual folly of her enterprise; for she was far more likely to perish than to succeed. She cast herself upon a sea of dangerous adventure, relying upon the resources of her affection; which, viewed apart from the casualty which saved her, were utterly insufficient for her purpose. She relied upon herself only because she was too ignorant to understand her own insufficiency. Her self-reliance, therefore, was more culpable than praiseworthy, — more likely to plunge her into ruin than to lead her to success. It lacked proper foundations. The qualifications necessary to make her advent into society in search of her knight successful were wanting; and, but for its favorable results, would be viewed as the rash enterprise of a love-sick girl.

A self-reliance equally rash is possible in my reader. She may rely upon herself, without reflecting on the real difficulties of life, or the inadequacy of her powers to combat them. With the weakness of the lamb, she may falsely deem herself able to contend against the strength of the lion. Confident in her abilities, she may go forth, like the emir's daughter; but no similar fortunate intervention of Providence may snatch her from danger, or hinder an army of difficulties from trampling her in the mire of misfortune and ruin. True self-reliance is cognizant of all the ills of earthly existence, and it rests on a rational consciousness of power to contend with them It counts the cost of the conflict with real life, and calmly concludes that it is able to meet the foes which stand, in frowning array, on the world's great battle-field. Such is the self-reliance whose necessity I urged in the preceding chapter, and whose secret springs I intend to describe in this.

One of these springs is a decided mind — an established purpose of the heart not to be turned aside from the path of duty by any consideration of pleasure, pain or profit.

A notable illustration of decision of character is found in the conduct of the rough but brave Pizarro, in his celebrated conquest of Peru. He and his warriors had already endured the most fearful sufferings and extreme privations. They had warred with nature in the vast solitudes of the Andes, — they had contended with the undisciplined but fierce bravery of the Indian native. Worn out by fatigue, prostrated through want of nourishment, condemned and recalled by their superiors at Panama, they stood, forlorn and discouraged, on the Isle of Gallo, resolved to return, and to abandon their enterprise. Then Pizarro stood forth in the greatness of his character. Tracing a line in the sand east and west, with the point of his sword, he turned towards the south and said, "Friends and comrades! on that side are toil, hunger, nakedness, the drenching rain, desertion and death; on this side, ease and pleasure. There lies Peru, with its riches; here, Panama, and its poverty. Choose each man what best becomes a brave Castilian! For my part, I go to the south!"

With these words, he crossed the line, followed by as many spirits as had caught the infectious energy of his speech. That act, so timely and characteristic, made him the conqueror of Peru.

The point I wish you to notice, in this incident, is, the consecration of life and fortune to a favorite idea which it manifests in Pizarro. He had deliberately weighed the dangers and the glory of his ideal conquest. He had devoted his life to its realization. Hence, the prospect of danger and death could not intimidate him, nor move him from his purpose. He preferred to die aspiring and contending for an empire, rather than to live an easy, inglorious life. This spirit made him invincible.

To enter life with safety, you require a corresponding consecration of life and fortune to *the idea of duty.* You must deliberately dedicate yourself to the claims of right. You must habituate yourself to resist every motive to wrong, whether it appeals to hope or fear, pain or profit; and to decide instantly, and finally, in all cases, great and small, in favor of right and truth. By such self-training, your moral instinct will acquire such quickness and strength, that it will be difficult to resist it, and easy to follow it. Right will become your guiding star. You will grow conscious of an adhesion to it so strong, that any measure of physical agony, or even death itself, will be preferable to a departure from its dictates.

With a mind conscious of such noble decision, — sure of itself in moments of temptation, — how justly may a young lady rely upon herself, when called by the providence of God to stand bereft of earthly supporters, on the bustling stage of life! Poverty, sorrow, toil, scorn, she may suffer; but shame, guilt and remorse, never. Her decision of character shields her from guilt, which is the worst of ills. With this security, she can afford to hurl defiance at all the rest. She may walk through fire, but she cannot be burned. Floods may roll around her, but she cannot be overwhelmed. She carries an amulet of mysterious power in her heart, and is safe.

I have often admired the decision of Josephine's affection for the emperor Napoleon. Notwithstanding his infamous cruelty in divorcing her for nothing but reasons of cold-hearted state policy, she never swerved for a moment from her attachment. Though separated from him, she cherished his image in her heart; brooded over the past with melancholy fondness; rejoiced in his success, and grieved over his fall. Though no one had been so greatly wronged, no one continued to love him with so pure a regard. No evil passion was permitted to break forth against him, — but he remained the idol of her heart, unti it broke with the swellings of anguish and sorrow.

It is from such a decided and incorruptible affection for the idea of duty, I would have the sentiment of self-reliance flow in my young reader's soul. Thus supported, she may gaze on the armed troops of temptations which frown upon her, and say, in the language of a bold general to his mutinous legions:

> "Put up your paltry weapons!
> They edgeless are to him who fears them not.
> Rocks have been shaken from their solid base, —
> But what shall move a firm and dauntless mind?"

Courage that shrinks not from the coming of danger, but bravely girds itself for assault and victory, is another secret spring of self-reliance in a young lady. A weak and timid spirit cowers and weeps, in imbecile fear, when evil rises frowning in her presence. But a courageous woman resembles that noble matron at Lexington, — Mrs. Harrington, — who, when the tramp of the British soldiers startled the ears of the patriots, and proclaimed the coming of war and death, instead of sitting down to tremble and shed useless tears, hurried to the foot of the stairway, and shouted to her sleeping son of sixteen

"Jonathan, you must get up; the regulars are coming. Something must be done!"

This is an example of genuine courage. It looked the danger in the face, and conceived a bold and settled purpose to assail it. Fear was subdued by the stern resolve to confront its object. The "regulars" were viewed not merely as messengers of death, but as the minions of royalty, to be driven back to Boston by patriotic valor. "SOMETHING" was to "BE DONE."

The young lady may imagine that in these days of peace courage is unnecessary in a woman. This is a mistake. Courage is as necessary to-day as in times of war or martyrdom. It is not battle-fields or scaffolds, alone, that try the soul and demand courage. Every-day life calls loudly for its exercise. Does it require no courage for that young lady, long nursed in the lap of indulgent kindness, who has just returned from her father's grave, to go forth into the world a penniless orphan? Can that mother, reared by kind parents in her girlhood, but left to support herself and little ones by a brutal husband, who nobly fulfilled all the early promise of his youth,

> "Till cursed passion
> Came like a sun-stroke on his mid-day toil,
> And cut the strong man down,"

and taught him to forget his vows, waste his means in profligate dens, and carry unmitigated abuse to his home, — can she dispense with courage? Can that widow, bereaved of her husband, and suddenly left in poverty, with helpless children to maintain, struggle with her lot without courage? Can woman minister to the sick, or endure her own heritage of sorrow, without it? Nay, young lady; courage is as necessary to you as to a warrior, — and without it you never can possess genuine self-reliance.

One important use of courage in woman is to inspire the spirit of her father, brother, husband or son, in the hour of trial. Some women sink, and drag their friends with them, in the hour of trouble. A father's difficulties are greeted with the tears of his wife and the lamentations of his daughters. They even reflect upon him, and charge his conduct with folly. Shame on such women! They pour the overflowing drop into a full cup. They tread upon the fallen one. They plunge the drowning victim beneath the wave. Such women are unworthy of their sex. Their spiritless conduct plucks down ruin upon themselves and on their households. When too late, they survey their wretched work, and gazing on the ruin they helped to create, they are forced to cry, with the VICTORIA of the tragic poet,

> "What have I done? I've fooled a noble heart—
> I've wrecked a brave man's honor!"

It is a woman's duty to cheer, not to depress; to encourage, not to alarm; to inspire with fresh spirit for renewed struggles against misfortune, not to plunge into despair and inactivity. How beautifully is this noble trait exemplified in the COUNTESS ALBERT, the wife of an Austrian nobleman! Before his marriage, he was guilty of fighting a duel with a general of the imperial army, in opposition to the express commands of the emperor. His shot took effect upon his opponent. He fled for his life, and was captured by a band of banditti which infested the Istrian forests. He was afterwards arrested, and sentenced to be broken alive upon the wheel at Vienna. But, upon his person and rank being discovered, his sentence was modified into one of perpetual banishment to the quicksilver mines of Idria.

The count was betrothed to a German lady, who belonged to one of the noblest families in the country. She was beautiful, educated and opulent, and had, in the circumstances of the count, reasons sufficient to satisfy an ordinary mind for dissolving their engagement. But her attachment was one of the highest and most exalted character. Instead of joining in the voices of censure that fell so freely and deservedly on the count, she exerted herself, to the utmost of her influence, to procure his liberation. Failing in this, she formed the extraordinary purpose of sharing his sufferings, and of cheering him by her presence in his toils. Thither she went, and in those dark, dismal mines, so unhealthy and so destructive of life, became his wife. There her cheerfulness sustained his spirit; her constant love calmed his soul; her voice animated him with hope. Magnanimous woman! What courageous love was hers, to brave the sentiment of the world, to face the horrors of an abode more gloomy than a prison, and to incur the certainty of a speedy death, that she might, by the lustres of her affection, irradiate the dreary heart of her husband!

In contrast with this unchiding devotion to a husband in misfortune, behold AYXA, the mother of ABO ABDELI, the Moorish monarch, as she stood by his side, on the hill of Padul, which overlooks Granada. The brave Ferdinand, with his chivalric Castilians, had just expelled him and his defeated troops from the city. He had lost his throne and his palaces, and could not avoid a flood of tears, as he gazed, for the last time, on the beautiful city which was no more to own him as its lord. The sultana beheld his sorrow, and addressed him in taunting words, saying:

"Thou dost well to weep, like a woman, over the loss of that kingdom which thou knewest not how to defend and die for, like a man!"

This bitter reproof was merited, for the king lacked the enthusiastic bravery which had characterized his ancestors; but it was not fitting to a mother's lips to utter it at that time. Doubtless it stung him deeply, increased his wretchedness, and added to his burdens, already too heavy to be borne. It was his mother's duty to stimulate his courage, by soothing his subdued spirit, — to awaken new hopes in his breast, and rouse his slumbering energies. This bitter vexation of the sultana places her at an immeasurable distance from the exalted, unrepining wife of the Austrian count.

Learn, then, young lady, to become the good, guardian genius of the opposite sex. Breathe hope, vigor, encouragement, into all hearts that live around you. But, to do this, you must be brave yourself. You require a strong, trustful, courageous spirit in your own breast. You need to carefully cultivate it, by subduing fear, and laboring to rise equal to your present emergencies. It is not fear alone, but fear unrestrained, that makes a coward; nor is bravery the absence of fear.

"The brave man is not he who feels no fear,
For that were stupid and irrational;
But he whose noble soul his fear subdues,
And bravely dares the danger nature shrinks from."

Nor is it necessary for you to be led into extraordinary circumstances, to learn or to practise courage. If it were, you might despair of acquiring it, since

"Small occasions in the path of life
Lie thickly sown, while great are rarely scattered."

Therefore, seek to be brave in the affairs of your girlhood. Overcome the timidity of your sex, by undaunted resolution to meet and conquer all difficulties that may arise, and you will be the possessor of a second element of self-reliance.

A third spring of this essential quality is a consciousness of ability to support yourself by the fruit of your own labor.

Listen to the advice of a noble Carolinian, Henry Laurens, who had nursed his daughters in the lap of luxury and refinement, but who, by the reverses of fortune, found himself a prisoner in the Tower of

London, during our Revolutionary war. Writing to his children, he said:

"It is my duty to warn you to prepare for the trial of earning your daily bread by your daily labor. Fear not servitude. Encounter it, if it shall be necessary, with the spirit becoming a woman of an honest and pious heart!"

I have said it before, but feel justified in saying again, that the experience of vast numbers of tried and suffering women justifies this judicious advice, and bids every young woman, whatever her condition may be, acquire some trade or skill by which she may be confident of earning her own bread. Nay, young lady, curl not that beautiful lip in proud contempt, though you are clad in silk and live in the halls of wealth; for in many a dark cellar and comfortless garret there toil, with weary fingers, the wrecks of women, who, in their youth, were proud and rich as you. The wheel of fortune has revolved, and, for plenty and ease, they have poverty and pain. You may suffer similar reverses. Courage to face a descent in the social scale you cannot have, unless you become mistress of some means of self-support, any more than a really brave man could be courageous amid armed bands, without a weapon of defence. As arms are necessary for the display of courage in a soldier, so is the consciousness of ability to live on the fruits of her personal industry essential to a woman of self-reliance.

But what can I do ? you inquire. Anything you attempt. But what should I attempt ? Everything within your reach. The intellectual Madame De Genlis could boast the possession of thirty various employments, by which, if necessary, she could earn her own living. You do not need so many modes as this ; but you may require, and can acquire, several, if you please. You can be very thorough in the acquisition of the elementary studies which are embraced in your educational course ; and thus, while fitting yourself to act well your part in society, you may also be gaining the power to live by teaching others. Do you pursue music, drawing, the languages, as accomplishments ? Be as perfect in them as possible ; use your knowledge by gratuitously instructing some humble friend or neighbor, and it will repay your toil with compound interest, in the day of your necessity; for a lady who is fully competent to teach, especially the ornamental branches of study, is almost sure to find profitable employment.

Your skill in needle-work may be turned to similar account. Learn to use your needle in the manufacture of every article that female fingers can construct. Do not be dependent on a milliner for your bonnet, nor upon a mantua-maker for your dress. Acquire their arts yourself. A few dollars will purchase all the instruction necessary. It is a shame for any young lady of ordinary abilities and good opportunities not to learn these simple arts. Even if she is pecuniarily above the need of using them, she should acquire them, and put them to charitable uses, — like that ancient matron, who made coats and dresses for the poor. Then, if the fiery hour of calamity overtake her, she is prepared to defy its flames. She has a fortune in her skill.

The factory is resorted to, by many young ladies,

as a suitable place to maintain themselves. Many of these possess superior abilities, and earn considerable sums of money; respectability, intellect, beauty, and high moral excellency, characterize them; nevertheless, my honest conviction is, that life in a cotton-mill is unfavorable to their best interests. The factory has not given them their superior qualities. These were acquired in the more congenial atmosphere of a happy home, and are nurtured, not by the influences of the cotton-mill, but in spite of them. The factory is unfavorable to a healthful, happy life. How can a young woman enjoy perfect health, for any length of time, who is confined in the hot, impure air of a spinning or weaving room, for nearly fourteen hours of every day? — who is allowed from twenty minutes to half an hour only to her meals, half of which has to be spent in going and returning? How can she cultivate either mind or heart, who is roused from her morning slumbers at half-past four or five o'clock, by the iron-mouthed bell, and who hurries, half awake, to her task, — at which she toils, wearily enough, until half-past seven at night? Even then, she has to take her supper; for, during the last six hours and a half of her toil, she tastes no food! What time, disposition or strength, has such a girl left for mental or religious culture? What opportunity to enjoy social pleasure? Is it surprising that the wheels of life drag heavily, under such circumstances? — that hundreds go, with broken constitutions, to their mountain homes, to die of lingering consumption? Nay, it is not wonderful. The wonder is, that the victims are not more numerous. I counsel you, therefore, young lady, to avoid the factory, if not in it; if already in it, leave it and become independent of it, by acquiring some more congenial means of self-support, before you resume your post. The time may arrive when the hours of factory toil will be abridged to some ten hours a day, and the compensation remain adequate to a respectable support. In that case, I might slightly vary my counsels. But, even then, I would urgently insist on the necessity of your having more than one means of living, so that you might be prepared for the emergencies of trying hours.

Do not think, from these hints, that I indulge or encourage any acrimonious sentiments towards mill-owners. Nay, I believe many of them to be humane, benevolent, godly men, who would willingly do for their help all that ought to be done. But such men do not control the system. Greedy capitalists, who care more for a rise in stocks than for human happiness or divine approval, — men, whose creed, learned in the temples of Mammon, teaches that

> "He best the doctrines Christ bequeathed fulfils,
> Who slays most hirelings and employs most mills,"

are the most guilty and responsible parties for the abuses of the factory system. They force many, against their wishes, to accept the system as it is, or to abandon it altogether. These are the men whose inhuman policy, of getting the largest amount of labor for the smallest amount of money, renders my advice necessary,—and they, too, are the men whom God will judge.

I need not add to these hints on self-support the

necessity of a thorough knowledge of domestic and household labor. Your own common sense teaches you how sadly embarrassed a dependent woman must be, who is unskilful in the arts of the kitchen and the laundry. Even at the head of a household with abundant means, such skill is indispensable to quietude and happiness. Your good sense also teaches you to despise the notion that such labors degrade a woman. She is degraded who cannot perform them; and even a poor ignorant Irish girl will despise a mistress whose household skill is beneath her own. Neither can you imagine that such duties are inconsistent with high intellectual culture and usefulness; for the lives of such gentlewomen as Madame ROLAND, who could prepare her husband's dinner with her own hands in the daytime, and in the evening attract the admiration of the greatest minds in France by her learned and brilliant wit; Mrs. MARY DWIGHT, the daughter of JONATHAN EDWARDS, who, while she performed her household duties with industry and propriety, also, by her great mental vigor, awakened the souls of her children to a love of letters and virtue, with a success which made her worthy to be the mother of such a son as TIMOTHY DWIGHT, — these, and scores besides, prove, beyond dispute, that devotion to household duties is not at variance with the cultivation of refined and liberal learning.

Seek, therefore, young lady, for skill in household labors; acquire some means of living by your own labor; cultivate a courageous spirit; learn to be decided in your adhesion to the voices of duty, — and you will be fitted to confront, with a consciousness of strength to overcome them, the most trying ordeals of life. Resting on these qualities, you will feel strong, your heart will be bold, you will not sink, with a crushed and broken spirit, under the pressure of difficulty, — but, erect and mighty, you will be mistress of your circumstances, and victor over your trials. Provided, however, you trust for the divine blessing on your personal attainments and efforts.

Behold an ancient Roman tribunal, with its venerable judges, its lictors, its councillors and its crowds of spectators. A man of benevolent countenance and lofty dignity stands at the bar. He casts his expressive eyes over the assembly, as if looking for some sympathetic face. An air of sadness suddenly darkening his features, proclaims his disappointment. Not one familiar friendly face is there. All have left him in his extremity. The sentence of that court may be the highest penalty of law, and his admirers and adherents are unwilling to risk their own liberties, by being present to encourage their friend. But see! the shadow departs. Light streams from his enraptured eyes, a lovely smile plays upon his lips, a rich glow irradiates his countenance. His bearing becomes more fitting to a triumphant conqueror than to a prisoner liable to a violent death. Who is he? What is he? Whence his power?

Reader, that man is PAUL THE APOSTLE, at the bar of imperial Rome, to answer for the offence of the cross. His converts had forsaken him, and for a moment he felt sad. That sudden change shall be explained by his own words to a beloved friend, to whom he wrote:

"*At my first answer, no man stood with me; but all men forsook me. Notwithstanding,* THE LORD STOOD WITH ME AND STRENGTHENED ME."

Here is the glorious secret. All his eloquence, his learning, his logical skill, were insufficient in that hour. He looked for further aid. He dared not rely wholly upon his gifts. But when his faith discerned the presence of God, to bless his gifts and control events, he felt sure. The ground became as solid rock beneath him. Learn, therefore, young lady, in addition to all other trusts, to lean on the aid of God. Look for his energy to operate through your gifts and attainments, and to give them their chief efficiency. Rest not, until you are able to say, "The Lord stands with me!" Then, though you are of all women most delicate, weak and exposed, you shall stand a pillar of invincible strength, defying alike the roaring of the waves and the howling of the wind. The springs of self-reliance will be in you indeed.

CHAPTER VIII.

OF SELF-CULTURE.

JOANNA BAILLIE has a tragedy named ETHWALD, whose hero is described as having, in his "fair opening youth,"

> " A heart inclined
> To truth and kindly deeds,
> Though somewhat dashed with shades of darker hue.
> But from this mixéd sea of good and ill,
> One baleful plant in dark strength raised its head,
> O'ertopping all the rest; which favoring circumstance
> Did foster up into a growth so monstrous,
> That underneath its wide and noxious shade
> Died all the native plants of feebler stem."

This passage unveils the heart of the reader, as fully as it does that of the poet's ideal hero. For, "as face answers to face in a glass;" so does one human heart to all others. In all there is a living seed of good deposited by that Almighty quickener, the Holy Ghost. In all, imperious passion, latent but potential, dwells like a torpid worm, awaiting the warmth of opportunity to awake and sting the soul, and to corrupt the budding fruits of virtue.

Out of this fact springs the duty and the necessity of self-culture. The soil of the human heart, and the aliment on which it is fed, are not only not favorable to the growth of the divine seed, but absolutely adverse to it, — while to the development of the destructive worm they are precisely adapted. Left to its own workings, the heart is as sure to warm its passions into a controlling life, and to hinder the vegetation of virtuous fruit, as a worm, lodged in a rose-bud, is to prevent its blooming to perfection. The holy seed, it is true, possesses an infinite energy, and a mysterious vigor. Nevertheless, it demands, as a condition of its growth, that, with careful and assiduous diligence, the passions should be trained, subdued and ruled, by the intellect and conscience of her who desires it to bear the unpurchaseable fruit of happiness and moral beauty. Nor is this a light task; for, as FLAVEL remarks, "It is much easier to pull many weeds out of a garden, than one corruption out of the heart, and to procure a hundred flowers to adorn a plot, than one grace to beautify a soul."

In extensive museums there are usually collected various specimens of marble statuary. The rudely-sculptured, grotesque figures of half-civilized art are there, looking like caricatures, rather than resemblances of any living thing. Ranging from these unseemly offsprings of an untutored genius, there are images in every stage of perfection and imperfection, up to the loveliest and highest creations of the artist, inspired by the purest conceptions of beauty. But all these varied forms were once unhewn and shapeless portions of the quarry. They owe their several differences of form and figure to the diversity of skill employed in giving them their respective shapes. Had the chisel of Canova or Chantrey wrought on the block of stone which ruder artists converted into a resemblance so obscure that the spectator can hardly decide whether it represents a monkey or a man, it had become a form so lifelike and beautiful as to awaken emotions of admiration, and sentiments of heroism, pity or love.

Society presents similar varieties of human character, and for reasons somewhat corresponding. One woman is *vain*, and answers the poet's description:

> " She who only finds her self-esteem
> In others' admiration begs an alms,
> Depends on others for her daily food,
> And is the very servant of her slaves."

Another is artful, capricious and unprincipled. Selfish and unlovely, she courts the love of others for her own advantage or pleasure. Finding herself despised a stream of bitter hate flows through her heart, — a pitiless tide of sorrow, which compels the cry,

> "But now the wave of life comes darkly on,
> And hideous passion tears my aching heart."

Others are given to slander; serpents, who

> "In the path of social life
> Do bask their spotted skins in Fortune's sun,
> And sting the soul! Ay, till its healthful frame
> Is changed to secret, festering, sore disease,
> So deadly is the wound."

Others, again, lack modesty, or sincerity, or purity of spirit. They are bold, false, ignorant and disgusting. On the other hand, there stand those women who are the models of their sex. Refined in feeling, pure in heart, gentle in manner, of noble and exalted minds, they command the admiration and secure the love of all beholders. They are lovely images of the divine ideal of woman; their character is the offspring of that sacred seed whose ripened fruit is a complete resemblance to Him who is the model of all human perfection.

All these women were substantially the same when as yet they lay cradled in maternal arms. Whence the difference in the years of their maturity? It lies in the diversity of their culture. While one class carefully repelled every evil motion of their spirits, and studiously cherished every desire for good, the other left the seed of good neglected, permitted their evil passions to gain strength by indulgence, until, like tares in a field of grain, they over run her soul. The lovely and the good are what they are through a faithful improvement of heavenly grace deposited within them; the evil are evil because they neglected such self-cultivating efforts.

Would my young reader belong to the model class of women? Does she desire to rank with those females whom God and man delight to honor? Then she must turn the eyes of her mind upon her self, as the sculptor gazes on a choice block of mar ble, and resolves to shape it into the beauteous ideal which is dimly floating in his mind. So, also, she must resolve, by the aid of grace, to make for herself a character in purity like the cherubim, and in loveliness like the seraphim.

But what if you have hitherto neglected this duty? If the seed of pride, of ambition, of unholy love or of bitter hate, has already germinated, and covered your soul with its dark and poisonous shadows? Is your case hopeless, therefore? Nay! Though by early culture the soul is most easily moulded to virtue, still it is never too late to improve it, so long as the mind retains strength to form a noble purpose. However conscious of unloveliness you may be, I summon you, nevertheless, to the sacred task of self-cultivation, in the language of JANE DE MONTFORT to her brother, who had yielded himself a slave to the passion of hatred:

> "Call up thy noble spirit,
> Rouse all the generous energy of virtue,
> And with the strength of Heaven-endued man
> Repel the hideous foe! Be great, be valiant!
> O, if thou couldst, e'en shrouded as thou art
> In all the sad infirmities of nature,
> What a most noble creature wouldst thou be!"

If a young lady is about to work a piece of embroidery, she is at great pains to procure the best of patterns. This she carefully studies, until she obtains a clear conception of the figures she is to produce by the magic of her own needle. Without this idea of her task, her production would probably be inferior and worthless.

Self-culture implies a similar apprehension of its end. A distinct vision of the work to be done, and how it is to be accomplished, must be before the mind, or every effort will be like an arrow aimlessly shot into the air. What, then, is the appropriate aim of all attempts at self-cultivation? Is it not the highest and most harmonious development of your entire being, physical, intellectual and moral? It comprehends the health of the body, the expansion of the intellect, the purification of the heart. It guards the health, because a feeble body acts powerfully on the mind, and is a clog to its progress. It cherishes the intellect, because it is the glory of a human being. It trains the moral nature, because, if that is weak or misdirected, a blight falls on the soul, and a curse rests upon the body. As each faculty reäcts favorably or unfavorably upon all the others, true self-culture attends with a due proportion of care to each. It strives to restrain one power whose action is too intense, and to stimulate another which is torpid. Thus by degrees the several faculties are balanced, — they act in delightful harmony with each other, and the result is the healthful progress of the person toward the highest point of attainable perfection.

Self-culture includes, as just stated, a proper care for the health of the body. So much has been written on this subject, that I forbear enlarging upon it, except to say, that a resolution to be careless of your health is a purpose to be both stunted in intellect and miserable in feeling. You might as wisely expect to enjoy life in a dilapidated and ruined habitation, which affords free admission to the freezing blast and the pitiless rain, as to be happy in a body ruined by self-indulgence. Is not the body the house of the soul? Can its mysterious tenant find rest and unmixed joy within its chambers, if daily exposed to sharp and shivering shocks through its aching joints or quivering nerves? Impossible! absolutely impossible! Attend, therefore, young lady, to your health, as a condition of happiness; and that you may do so successfully, consult your common sense in relation to many popular injurious habits, and some simple work on physiology, that you may learn those laws of your physical organization, upon whose observance so much of the true pleasure of life depends.

Self-culture also implies suitable efforts to strengthen and expand the intellect, by reading, by reflection, and by writing down your thoughts. Reading suitable books stores the mind with facts and principles; reflection converts those facts and principles into a real mental aliment, and thus quickens the soul into growth; while writing tends to precision of thought and beauty of expression. Every young lady should, therefore, read much, reflect more, and write as frequently and carefully as she has opportunity.

The principal object of reading, with most young persons, is pleasure. They seek for excited sensibilities and a charmed imagination. Hence, novels and poetry form the staple of their reading. Grave history, graver science, and dull philosophy, they eschew, while they actually abhor the sober pages of theology. The novel is well thumbed; the poem, if it is not too Miltonic, is well turned down at the corners; but poor Gibbon, Mosheim, Newton, Buffon Butler, Blair and Wesley, lie quietly in some snug corner, robed in cobwebs, beside the dust-covered and despised Bible. What is the consequence? Obscured, feeble intellect, a weakened memory, an extravagant and fanciful imagination, benumbed sensibilities, a demoralized conscience, and a corrupted heart! A troop of evils more to be dreaded by a young lady than the advance of an invading army, — for soldiers only kill the body, but these strangle the immortal mind.

Would you admit a thief to your cabinet of jewels? Would you invite a base profligate to your society? Nay. The question itself pains you. Pardon me, lady, — I would not willingly inflict the slightest wound on your spirit, — but I must deal frankly with you, or forfeit my claims of friendship. Hearken, therefore, to my statement. If you are an indiscriminating novel reader, you admit both thieves and profligates, not merely to your society, but to your most intimate companionship, — yea, into the palace of your soul. Novels rob you of a higher pleasure than they afford, since the same attention to solid reading would procure you a loftier, purer pleasure. Hence, they are thieves who rob you of real delight. Then, what are their heroes, chiefly, but villains, robbers, profligates and murderers? These you take to your fellowship, listen to their language, grow interested in their adventures, and imbibe a portion of their spirit; for all this is necessarily implied in the devotion with which your tossed and excited mind follows them in the windings of their history. Can your soul be a bright mirror, in which none but pure images are reflected, after such reading? Can they leave you wholly free from sympathy with impure thought? Can you escape contamination? Nay. As soon might the mirror be undimmed in the densest fog, or a person walk undefiled through an overflowing ditch.

Novels are also injurious to your religious interests. They create a loathing at the bare idea of a spiritua. life, and bind you in chains to a life of sin. They fit you to resist the awakenings of the Holy Spirit. A love for them often becomes the rallying-point or conflict between Christ and sin. As, in a certain revival, two persons were awakened who were inveterate novel readers. Their favorite books stood in the way of their conversion. They were willing to be Christians, if their idol could remain undestroyed. This, of course, was impossible, and they saw it. One of them yielded, gave up her novels, and became a joyful convert. The other determined to cleave to her favorite books, whether she obtained religion or not, and was soon freed from serious feelings. She preferred novels to Christ, and Christ forsook her! Nor is she alone. Thousands have made the same choice, and have experienced a similar fate. Reader, will you abandon novels? By all your desire for intellectual and moral improvement, I beg you to forsake them at once, wholly, and forever.

When you read, you should do so for the purpose of gaining knowledge, or to invigorate your intellect, or to stimulate your moral faculties, according to the character of the book before you. In either case, do not hasten over the paragraphs as the high-mettled racer rushes along the course. After every sentence, pause, close your eyes, or lift them from the book, and repeat your author's thought in your mind. Inquire if you understand his meaning, if he states the truth, or if he reasons correctly. Then proceed to the next sentence, and repeat this mental process. In this way, you will taste a hitherto unknown pleasure, and derive vast profit from the books you read. As to the best books for your use, you had better consult some judicious friends. Your parents, your pastor, or your teacher, will give you all necessary advice on this point.

There is no book so well adapted to improve both the head and the heart as the Bible. It is a *tried* book: its utility is demonstrated by experience; its necessity is confessed by all who have studied the wants of human nature; it has wrung reluctant praises from the lips of its foes. Adopt it for your daily companion. Read it thoroughly, patiently, carefully. Read a portion of it daily, on your knees, pausing at each sentence, and asking its great Author to teach you its import, to stamp it on your heart, and to make it a means of life and health to your soul. Do this, and you will shortly learn to set a price upon its worth far above the costliest rubies.

Your *moral* faculties also demand the most careful attention. Indeed, your first and principal care must be in this direction, since your happiness depends more upon their healthful condition than upon the state of your body and intellect. With disordered moral faculties, you will be as a ship without a helm, dashed on bars and rocks, at the will of winds and waves.

The secret of moral self-culture lies in training the will to decide according to the fiat of an enlightened conscience. When a question of good or ill is brought before the mind for its action, its several faculties are appealed to. The intellect perceives, compares, and reflects on the suggestions. The emotions, desires and passions, are addressed, and solicited to indulgence. The conscience pronounces its verdict of right or wrong, on the proposed act. Then comes the self-determining will, coinciding either with the conscience or the emotions. The end of right moral culture is to habituate it to decide against the passions, desires and emotions, *whenever they oppose the conscience,* — thus establishing the supremacy of divine claims over the soul.

The "magician of the north," Sir WALTER SCOTT, has made the name of JEANIE DEANS a household word. The real name of this noble girl was Helen Walker, the orphan daughter of a Scottish farmer. Her younger sister, ISABELLA, whom in childhood she had supported by her own industry, and whom she tenderly loved, was arrested for the murder of her babe, born out of wedlock. When the day of trial arrived, Helen was told that her sister's life was in her power. If she would testify that she had known Isabella to make even the slightest preparations for its birth, the scale would turn in her favor, and her life be saved from the gallows. All her sisterly affection, all her family pride, all her fear of the prospective ignominy growing from a connection with an executed felon, were thus appealed to. But her sense of duty triumphed. Without a moment's hesitation, she gave this lofty answer:

"It is impossible for me to swear to a falsehood; and, whatever may be the consequence, I will give my oath according to my conscience."

Noble woman! How supreme was the authority of duty in her soul! Between a temptation and a wrong volition in her mind, there stood a stern IMPOSSIBILITY! That her decision sprang from any lack of strong sisterly affection, cannot be imagined. Her heroic journey on foot from Scotland to London, her plea for her sister's life, when, clad in her simple plaid, she gained an audience before the Duke of Argyle, and her pure joy at her sister's pardon, combine to place this question beyond dispute, and to prove that her decision was the offspring of a will trained to acknowledge the supremacy of conscience.

Let us place Helen in contrast with another woman, whose character, in many respects, deserves much praise. I mean the Princess ELIZABETH, sister to the unfortunate King Louis of France. When the Parisian mob broke into the royal palace, they demanded the head of the queen, whom they hated most sincerely. "Where, where is she? We will have her head!" was their terrible question, as they met the princess in one of the chambers.

"I am the queen," replied Elizabeth.

"She is not the queen," cried her attendants, as they rushed forward to rescue her from their murderous hands.

"For the love of God," exclaimed the princess, "do not undeceive these men! Is it not better that they should shed my blood than that of my sister?"

The self-devotion of this act is certainly admirable; but its morality sinks far into the shade, beside the resplendent truthfulness of Jeanie Deans. It was noble to offer her life to save a sister, but not right to violate the law of truth for that purpose. The answer of the lost Constantine, in Joanna Baillie's tragedy, to Valeria, when she hinted her purpose not to survive his death, is in point here. To her he said,

"It is not well, it is not holy. No!
O no, my noble love, mine honored love!
Give to thy fallen lord all that the soul
To widowed love may give. But oh, stop there!"

The deceit of the princess merits the same reply, and proves that her will was not completely subjected to the control of an enlightened conscience.

Here, then, you discover the nature of your great and difficult work. And is it not a high and worthy task to place God and right on the throne of the soul? Will you not engage in it with all the vigor of your spirit — with all the might of your nature? If you say "I will," then suffer me to add, that you must diligently enlighten your conscience by the study of God's law, and strengthen your will by constant efforts, in the daily acts of life, to subordinate the feelings to its decisions. You must never permit a feeling, even if harmless, to grow into a controlling impulse; for just in proportion as impulses strengthen, the will is weakened and overborne. Hence the impulses must be habitually restrained by the commands of the will.

To illustrate my meaning; suppose yourself sailing in a boat. A sudden flaw of the wind causes her to lurch, so that the gunwale is almost submerged. You feel an impulse arising from your fears to spring to the opposite side of the boat. By doing so, you increase the danger, and probably capsize the boat. Or, you are riding in a carriage The driver leaves his seat. The reins are beyond your reach. The horses move on without a driver. You are alarmed. An impulse moves you to scream and hold out your arms for aid. Your screams set the horses into a run, and what might have been remedied, had you been silent, becomes a sad, ruinous disaster. In either case, you should resist your impulse; restrain it by a resolute refusal to submit to it. You can do this, for there is not a faculty of mind or body which the will is not capable of controlling. But it is only by habituating the mind to reflect, and the will to command, on right principles, in all things great and small, that its power can be established. And, in moral self-culture, this is the grand point to which your mightiest efforts must be directed.

One condition of success, in all endeavors after self-improvement, is the avoidance of everything which tends to strengthen evil dispositions or desires.

DRESS, for example, by being ornamental and fashionable fosters pride and vanity, is unfavorable to economy, occupies too much time, and leads to many other ills. *Dancing*, *cards*, and other fashionable amusements, awaken the various passions, weaken the power of conscience, and create a positive disrelish for the sober pursuits and graver ends of human life. What, then, will self-culture avail, if these things are not given up? You might as easily extinguish a fire, which is fed by streams of oil, with tiny cups of water, as to restrain the growth of your propensities, while indulging in sinful amusements and silly fashions. To gain moral distinction and serene joy, you must wholly abandon the former; and in regard to the latter, simplicity and neatness are more tasteful and beautiful than ornament and show. She who would acquire the highest and most attractive loveliness must walk by the rule of those ancient women "who trusted in God," and after the counsels of Peter, who said to the women of his age:

"*Whose adorning let it not be that outward adorning of plaiting the hair, and of wearing of gold, or*

of putting on of apparel; but let it be in THE ORNA MENT OF A MEEK AND QUIET SPIRIT."

Imagine the spectacle of a light boat floating gayly over a wide sunlit sea. Its sole passenger is a lovely lady who appears to be suddenly wakening from sleep. Her hand is stretched out to grasp the string of a magnificent pearl necklace, which, during her sleep, became unfastened. One end is still hanging about her neck, the other is loosely dangling over the water. Pearl after pearl has slipped off into the deep abyss, until there are but few remaining. The expression on the lady's brow is sad and self reproachful. Each lost pearl reproves her; each remaining one reminds her of those which are gone while several more must fall, before her hand can reach the string to save the small remainder.

Do you perceive the IDEA embodied in this beauti ful spectacle? It is, that if the opportunities of early life for self-improvement are wasted in idle day-dreams, the loss can never be repaired. Lost opportunities are sunken pearls. Young life spent

in self-neglect will bring self-reproach in later years. Then you will cry,

> "Untaught in youth my heart to tame,
> My springs of life were poisoned."

Spend your early years in frivolous pleasures, and at your tomb it shall be said of you,

> "Her life had been quaffed too quickly, and she found
> The dregs were wormwood!"

Begin, therefore, young lady, to labor upon yourself with a diligence worthy of so great an end. Aim to develop yourself physically, intellectually, and morally, to the extent of your ability. Do it, depending on the grace of Jesus Christ, — or, as St. Paul says, "*looking unto Jesus;*" for, without Christ, you "*can do nothing.*" Begin to-day, for this is your only certain opportunity.

> "This moment
> Is precious as the life of man! Who knows
> If from the Judge's hand already fall not
> The last scant drops for thee?"

CHAPTER IX.

THE YOUNG LADY AT HOME.

THERE is not a female name in history that reflects so much dishonor on your sex as the Roman TULLIA, the wife of LUCIUS TARQUINIUS. She left no natural tie unviolated, that she might accomplish her ambitious purposes. A sister, a husband and a father, were sacrificed to her passion. But the crowning act of her vileness was the shameful indignity with which she treated her father's dead body. It lay across the street, weltering in blood. Her charioteer reined up his horses, lest he should drive them over the royal corpse. "Drive on!" cried the incensed Tullia, in a voice which made the horrified driver tremble. He obeyed; and, as the wheels of her chariot bounded over the corpse, the father's blood spirted upon the daughter's dress. The Romans expressed their horror of this inhuman, unfilial act, by naming the street *Vicus Sceleratus*, or Wicked Street. Her name is synonymous with infamy, in the mind of every reader of ancient history.

I know you shrink disgusted from her character. Every humane and filial feeling in your breast revolts at her image. This is well. But it does not prove you wholly free from some participation in a crime like hers. Not that I surmise you to bear the smallest degree of resemblance to her in cruelty or inhumanity. No. You have too much refinement of feeling, tenderness, and self-respect, for such a supposition. But Tullia's crimes are crimsoned by the fact of their being committed against a sister, a husband, a father. She stifled the sweetest voices of her nature. She crushed the dearest affections of the heart. She trampled upon the strongest ties that bind human beings together. She immolated

within herself, every beauty of the soul, that she might gratify the insatiate demands of her ambition. And may not these things be done by young ladies who shiver at the bare recital of the mode through which she displayed the workings of her unfilial and unsisterly heart? What shall be said of that daughter who treats a mother with contempt, and a father with disregard? What of her, who idly wastes her time, and leaves an aged or a feeble mother to toil unaided in domestic duties? What of her, whose insufferable temper destroys the happiness of the family circle, who tyrannizes over her brothers and sisters, whose wastefulness and vanity exhaust a father's means, and burden him with care that crushes his soul? Or of her, who, despising all parental counsel and authority, wilfully and blindly rushes into forbidden and dangerous society, thereby inflicting pangs more painful than the dagger's stroke upon the anguished spirits of her father and mother? Are such young ladies wholly free from the sin of Tullia? Nay! She violated filial and sisterly ties; they do the same. Thus far they resem-

ble each other. And there are some, whose secret conduct so poisons the springs of life in their parents, as to hurry them prematurely and sorrowfully to the grave. Such girls certainly partake largely of Tullia's spirit, and justly merit the severest reprobation. Earth has no more hateful object than an unfilial child; nor is there anything which the sentiment of mankind so severely censures and despises as ingratitude in a daughter. When known, she is

"Scorned, hooted, mocked!
Scorred by the very fools who most admired
Her worthless heart."

On the cther hand, how beautiful is filial love! How admirable is a daughter's gratitude! Behold an affecting example, in a scene that occurred some seventy years ago. See, in a scantily furnished chamber, a patriarchal man, with his wife, an aged and feeble dame. On both, time has set deep seals. Their faces are wrinkled, their hair is gray, the palsy of feebleness is on their limbs, and they sit upon their straight-backed chairs, dependent on the attentions of an only daughter.

And there she sits in gloomy silence, gazing on the cheerless grate. She is young, but grave beyond her years. Why is she so sad? Alas! she has ample reason for sorrow. Her hands have been the support of her parents; but it is a season of public distress, and work has failed. The last crust has been eaten, the last stick of wood burned, the last penny expended. Dread starvation stares her and her parents in the face. But see! A ray of sunshine darts from her tearful eyes. Her face lights up, for a thought of love has suddenly found birth in her heart. With silent haste she rooes herself in her well-worn shawl, and leaves the chamber. Let us follow her.

Her steps are rapid, and directed toward the principal street of the city. She pauses before a dentist's office. She had heard that he had offered three guineas for every sound front tooth that the owner would permit him to extract. Her loving heart had determined to sacrifice her teeth to save her aged parents from death, and she is here to bear the pain. Entering the office, she offers the dentist all her front teeth, at three guineas for each tooth.

"But why do you sacrifice all your front teeth, young lady?" the dentist inquires, astonished that so young and pretty a girl, should make such a proposal.

With a fluttering heart, she tells her simple story, fearful lest the dentist should refuse to make the purchase. Fortunately, he is a man of feeling. His heart is touched,— tears fill his eyes; he opens his purse, gives her ten guineas, and refuses to touch a single tooth. Filial love has conquered, and the happy daughter hastens to comfort the desponding spirits of her aged parents.

Behold yet one more example. An aged man was in the hands of the revolutionary murderers at Paris, and the sword was already uplifted to destroy him. Rushing through the mob, his daughter, Mademoiselle de Sombreuil, threw herself upon his neck, and cried,

"Hold your hands, barbarous wretches! He is my father!" And then she pleaded, with floods of tears, and with all the eloquence of love, for his life. A monster in the besotted crowd cried out,

"Drink the blood of the aristocrats, and save your father!"

The girl shuddered at this revolting proposal, and instinctively retreated a few paces. But the savage glances of the mob assured her that her venerable father must perish, unless she accepted the loathsome conditions. The test was terrible, but love triumphed. She took the proffered glass, and swallowed its contents. Her father was saved.

Such heroic love as this commands your highest admiration. It should stimulate you to its imitation. Not that you will ever have opportunity for such extraordinary proofs as these two ladies gave of their affection; but you are bound to manifest the same spirit, in all your deportment toward your parents. You should study to anticipate and obey their slightest wishes; address them in tones and words of respectful affection; never disgrace yourself by uttering an unkind word to either of them; make them your confidants; keep nothing secret especially from your mother; consult them concerning your plans, studies, amusements, and friends; relieve your mother as much as possible, by rendering her assistance in household labors to the very limit of your ability; never permit yourself to be disagreeable or resentful to your brothers and sisters, and study to find your own pleasure in promoting the happiness of the family circle. Thus will filial affection grow strong and beautiful in your soul. Your home will be sweet and delightful. Your parents will rejoice over you, as an olive plant of valued loveliness, and you will be fitted to make those heroic sacrifices, if the exigency should ever occur, which have immortalized the names of RUTH, of ELIZABETH the exile's daughter, of SOMBREUIL's child, and of other illustrious women. Your Creator will also hold you in remembrance for your fidelity to filial obligations. God loves a faithful child, and has condescended to incorporate his high regard for such in the "commandment with promise:" "*Honor thy father and mother, that thy days may be long in the land which the Lord thy God giveth thee.*"

Another duty that claims your attention, with imperial authority, is the cultivation of proper affections for your brothers and sisters. The tie that binds you to them is a precious, golden link in the chain of life, and should be preserved unbroken. Discord between childen of the same parents is the perfection of youthful misery. Envy, jealousy, bickering, are horrible monsters in any home; for their devastating appetites will devour every fruit of household bliss. On the contrary, fraternal and sisterly love is a soft, gentle star of beauty, in the domestic heavens. The voices of such affections are bewitching melodies, enchanting the soul by their bird-like tones. It is impossible to measure the amount of pleasure or misery, in a family, procured by the lovingness or hatefulness of its sons and daughters.

Be kind, therefore, young lady, to your brothers and sisters; and especially so, if you are an eldest daughter. Be unselfish and attentive. Exert yourself to please them, so that you may strike a chord of delight whenever they approach you. Encourage them in their studies and amusemen s. Gently check any wrong manifestation of character, both in them and in yourself. By these means, you will wind cords of enduring affection round their hearts. They will love you, and they will also love home for your sake. And, if your brother should be lured into the tempestuous seas of passion, your image, gleaming through the surrounding mists and vapors, will revive the strength of his virtue, and inspire him with the energy to escape from those foaming breakers where so many strong men have perished. Many a brother has fallen for lack of such a vision. A distasteful home has driven him into sinful society.

> "His father's house
> Has unto him become a cheerless den.
> His pleasant tales, and sprightly, playful talk,
> Which once their social meals were wont to charm,
> Now visit them but like a hasty beam
> Between the showery clouds."

Parents and sisters lament this sad alienation. Had they, by mutual affection, made their home a miniature paradise, — had his sister clothed herself in the angelic loveliness of sisterly affection, — he might still have been the household joy. But if not, how ennobling to her character would have been the consciousness of entire blamelessness for his fall!

Therefore, I say again, be as an angel of goodness to your brother. Treat him with forbearing kindness, resembling DE MONTFORT'S sister, who, having followed his restless steps to his retreat, and finding him amused at a mixed assembly, refused to be announced, saying,

> "I am his sister, —
> The eldest daughter of his father's house, —
> Calm and unwearied is my love for him;
> And, having found him, patiently I 'll wait,
> Nor greet him in the hour of social joy,
> To dash his mirth with tears."

The skilful horticulturist, in preparing young trees to enrich his orchard or beautify his grounds, keeps them, at first, in some congenial nook, where they are sheltered from the winds and frosts. When at a proper degree of maturity, they are transplanted to some other spot, to brave the winds and to bear fruit. And it pleases the Divine Husbandman to treat his creatures with an analogous but more loving consideration. He does not expose them suddenly to the bleak winds and sharp frosts of life, but places them in a downy nest, called home, where, duly sheltered, they may acquire power, experience, and wisdom, to go forth and boldly dare the severer responsibilities of life.

Therefore, home should be viewed as a social nursery, within whose protecting walls a young lady must fit herself for a higher and more difficult sphere. It is the place of opportunity; the dressing-room of life; the antechamber leading into the great hall of assembly, in which she is bound to enact some more or less important part.

How beautifully fitted is this blessed arrangement to the contemplated end! Home, "sweet, sweet home!" we may indeed call it; for there never was nor will be any other "place like home."

> "The parted bosom clings to wonted home,
> If aught that's kindred cheer the welcome hearth."

Home frees you from all care for present self-sustenance, and thus leaves your mind free for study and self-improvement. Home has voices of experience and hearts of genuine holy love, to instruct you in the ways of life, and to save you from a sense of loneliness, as you gradually discover the selfishness of mankind. Home has its trials, in which are imaged the sterner struggles of your after years, that your character may gain strength and manifestation; for which purpose they are necessary. They "open the portals of the heart, that its jewels, otherwise concealed in its hidden depths, may shine forth and shed their lustre on the world." Home has its duties, to teach you how to act on your own responsibility. Home gradually and gently increases its burdens, so that you may acquire strength to endure without being overtasked. Home is a little world, in which the duties of the great world are daily rehearsed. And so perfect is the adaptation of home, that if a young lady learns its lessons well and truly, she cannot well fail of fitness for any subsequent station which God may call her to fill. A dutiful daughter, a loving sister, an industrious girl, will make a happy wife, a good mother, and a valuable woman. Fidelity to the duties of her girlhood fits her for a glorious and blissful womanhood; while the undutiful daughter, the ill-tempered sister, the idle girl, whose pride is in the whiteness of her hands and the ornaments of her apparel, will as certainly grow into an odious wife, a foolish mother, or a lazy, disgusting woman.

Be faithful, therefore, young lady, to the calm and priceless opportunities afforded you in the pleasant home of your youth. They are golden seeds of golden fruit. Sow them assiduously, and sow them carefully. The harvest-time will surely come with smiles and gladness. Among the sheaves will be a husband's admiring love, a brother's gratitude, perhaps a child's affection. There, too, will be sheaves of rich reflections. As you gaze upon the past, the venerable faces of your departed parents will rise, distinct and smiling, among the dim and cloudy images of the mind. How delightful it will be to gaze, and to remember a loving, faithful past; to recall no unkind word, act, or look; but to feast on the thought of those affectionate interchanges of mutual kindness, which caused those well-remembered faces to look with ineffable love upon you! How delicious, how real, are such remembrances! Hear the poet describing a lady musing thus upon her early life. He says:

"As some fair lake reflects, when day is o'er,
With stiller deeps and clearer tide the shore,
So night and calm the lengthening memory glassed,
And from the silence rose distinct the past:
Again she sees her mother's gentle face;
Again she feels the mother's soft embrace;
Again the mother's sigh of pain she hears,
And starts — and lo! the spell dissolves in tears!"

Blessed tears! provided they are tears that come swelling from a precious tide of love, and not from the overflowing of a remorseful spirit. Dear lady, be faithful to the present hour! And, that you may have the power to be so, give Christ your heart. Let him purify your affections, and guide your spirit. Then will your experience justify the poet's exclamation of

"How the home brightens where the heart presides!"

CHAPTER X.

THE YOUNG LADY FROM HOME.

NOTWITHSTANDING all the voices of wisdom which fall on childish ears, in the sweet little home-world, where the young heart so fearlessly nestles, our first lessons of life are usually inaccurate; our first impressions of its character and duties obscure and false. Peeping out at the windows of our early home, we see the big world, as a traveller sees a landscape by the light of a waning moon, through pale, midnight vapors, and it appears to us a romantic scene of beauty only, fitted solely for our pleasure. But, as the rising sun wears the fog into "shreds and rifted masses," whose openings give "glimpse after glimpse of slow revealed" reality to the wanderer, so does an actual entrance into life gradually unfold, to a reflective young lady, the great truth, that the immutable law which forces her into the theatre of social life, aims to constitute her an *actor* on its stage, and not a mere pleased *spectator* of its shifting scenes. She learns, at least she may, if she is true to her opportunities, that she has a useful part to perform in the great drama of existence. That a constant, personal approximation towards the all-perfect, and a ceaseless endeavor to communicate good to others, are the sublime aims and duties proper to every human being! Happy is that young lady whose perception of this truth is clear, and whose adherence to it is firm and immovable! Let her follow it, as seamen the beaming of the northern star, or as the ancient magi the mystic star of the Saviour, and it shall guide her to the throne of Messiah, — to Him " who is over all, God blessed forever "!

As the academy is often the first sphere in which a young lady is called to lean somewhat upon herself, a few counsels, to regulate her life at school, may not be improper. I will, therefore, first present one important end of school education, by giving a somewhat humorous extract from the imaginative JEAN PAUL Describing the griefs of one of his characters, he says:

"SIEBENKAS pored over a fatal iron mould,—a mark or wart in his wife's heart. He could never raise her to a lyrical enthusiasm, in which she might forget heaven, and earth, and all things. She could count the strokes of the clock between his kisses, and listen to the pot boiling over, with the big tears, which he had drawn forth by a beautiful story, or a discourse from the outpourings of his heart, yet standing in her eyes. She sat in the adjoining room, and sang to herself quavering psalms, and in the middle of a verse she interpolated the prosaic question, 'What shall I cook this evening?' And he could never forget, that once, in the midst of a most moved attention to a closet-sermon of his, on death and eternity, she looked thoughtfully downwards, and at length said,

"'Don't put on your left stocking, to-morrow morning. I must first mend a hole in it!'"

Poor Siebenkäs! With what pain must he have cast away his manuscripts, when called from the height of sublime reflection to the ridiculous depth of a darned stocking! His wife was not blameworthy for her domesticity, but for the want of that high appreciation of the wealth of thought, — that literary sensibility and mental culture, — by which, in a leisure hour, she might have soared with her husband into the glowing regions of an elevated, ideal world, untrammelled, for the time, by thoughts of cooking and darning. For, to quote Jean Paul again, every woman should be capable of soaring to a certain height. She should be a woman on whose opened eyes and heart the flowery earth and beaming heavens strike, not in infinitesimals, but in large and towering masses; for whom the great whole is something more than a nursery-room or a ball-room. Her feelings should be at once tender and discriminating, and her heart at once pious and large.

To impart this discrimination, — this intellectuality, — this largeness of soul, — this noble sympathy with the great and beautiful, — is the work of education; the aim of your literary instructors. They would save you from the ridiculous littleness of the lady whose mind had closer sympathy with the darning-needle and the scullery than with those great thoughts that stir the truly elevated mind. They would not create any distaste for domestic life, — that were both sinful and foolish; but they would so expand your intellect, that in the spare, lonely, or social hours of after-life, you may live in a world of pure and blessed thought, — be fit for the companionship of superior minds; and escape that awful ennui, — that loathsome sense of soul-weariness, — which is the torment of uncultivated women.

This is a serious aim, and you must seriously entertain it, and enter thoroughly into it, or it cannot be accomplished. You must view the laborious struggle with crooked conjugations, difficult definitions, and perplexing theories, as having a positive relation to it. You must regard every fully digested lesson as a certain step toward a larger mental world. The grandeur of this idea will stimulate you when wearied, restrain you when attracted to improper objects, and sustain you in the little trials and self-denials of school-life. It will spur you to ascend every hill of difficulty, and cheer your struggles in every valley of confusion. It will make you the pride of your preceptors, and the model of your fellow-scholars. Your parents will feel repaid for the expenses of your education, and you will reap a rich harvest of enjoyment all the way through life.

Perhaps, my reader, you are one of those who find the acquisition of learning to be very difficult. You pursue it reluctantly, indolently, and almost hopelessly. This is wrong; for no young lady should ever be discouraged with herself, or despair of making indefinite improvement. You have elements of unknown power in your soul, and persevering, hopeful effort will draw them forth. Never despair of acquiring any study you earnestly enter upon, for you can acquire it if you will. Study, therefore, with cheerful diligence, — with faith in yourself, — and you shall, at length, rejoice in the consciousness of victory. Where would have been the unequalled triumphs of the peerless JENNY LIND, but for her persevering energy? Deprived of the control of her voice, just as it was winning green laurels for her childish brow; discouraged by the predictions of Garcia, he musical instructor, who dismissed her with the remark that "she had made great progress under his tuition, and should her voice fully return, he would prophesy her success; but of this he could see no prospect;" triumphed over by Mademoiselle Nissen, her rival at Berlin, this amiable songstress had difficulties enough to crush an ordinary mind. But she had the indomitable energy of true genius, and persisted in the severest endeavors to recover her voice, and to attain the highest artistical power to direct it. She had her reward. Her voice came, at last, as suddenly as it had left her. She felt conscious of her victory, and appeared before the audience with a radiant countenance. They had heard her often, and expected no surprise; but when she struck her first note, on that eventful night, every ear was ravished; and as she poured forth the gushing flood of music, they were enraptured, and, with bursts of admiration, they proclaimed her the "Queen of

Song." She deserved her triumph, because she had earned it by the self-denying discipline of years. Therefore, I say, young lady, persevere! You may not be formed for such transcendent excellence as some of the more highly gifted of your sex, but you are capable of unlimited improvement.

As to school manners, they are, or should be, the same as in any other circle of society. Ill manners in an academy or among its associations, are as disgusting and blameworthy as in any other place. They do their possessor much harm, for the evil character thus acquired at school often cleaves to a lady through life. Cultivate good manners, therefore, with as much assiduity as if you moved in a court circle. Only *feel* kind toward all, — have a sincere wish to impart pleasure to all you meet; be modest, be unassuming, be humble, and you cannot fail being well-mannered; for the most refined courtesies are those which proceed from a sincere and gentle spirit. Such a spirit, animating your intercourse with others, will color all your conduct with propriety, and prepare you for association with teachers or scholars, rich or poor, village coteries or city assemblies. Be careful, therefore, of your dispositions, and they, with a little common sense, will regulate your manners far better than all the foppish dancing-masters in existence.

I have already spoken of that necessity of exerting good or evil influence which is immutably linked to your existence, and of your *duty* to exert only a good influence over others. A benevolent spirit toward society, manifested in habitual acts of kind endeavor to benefit its members, is, therefore, not merely a question of choice, but a fearful obligation resting upon you. You form a part of the human family, that you may diminish its miseries and add to its pleasures. By a smile, a tear, a word, or a gift, you may daily send a beam of gladness into the sad spirit of some forsaken child of sorrow. By making this a principal object of your daily life, you will answer the grand end of social life, and your efforts will flow back upon your own soul in swelling seas of perennial joy.

An oriental ascetic, who had taken up his lonely

abode in the desert, was accustomed to carry water, in a glass, from a spring in his hermitage, to the weary travellers who passed his door. For this they blessed his habitation, as an oasis in the sandy waste. At last he bethought himself that it would be better to dig a well in front of his house, that the travellers of the desert might, even for ages after his death, freely slake their thirst. He obeyed the suggestion of his heart; and for generations the caravans paused at his well, and rejoiced in his far-reaching benevolence.

Even thus it should be, young lady, with you and your deeds of kindness. While, by private acts of love, you resemble the hermit bringing the single glass of water from his bubbling spring, you should, by lending your influence to the church of Christ and its various institutions, aid to perpetuate living fountains of public beneficence, to the latest ages of time.

There is no mode of benevolent action more suited to a young lady, than to labor as a teacher in a Sabbath-school. The beauty, the greatness, and the blessedness of this delightful work, are well expressed in the following lines, which I quote for your careful study.

> "'T is a fond, yet a fearful thing to rule
> O'er the opening mind in a Sabbath-school.
> Like wax, ye can mould it in the form ye will;
> What ye write on the tablet remains there still:
> And an angel's work is not more high
> Than aiding to form one's destiny."

The distribution of tracts, visiting the sick poor, aiding to sustain seamen's bethels and homes, and all kindred tasks, are also admirable spheres of benevolent action. Only be careful of associations of ultra reformers, — of men and women who decry all existing good, in their blind devotion to a particular idea. Such persons are like hunters, who, to capture a wicked fox, will trample down a field of valuable wheat, — and these pseudo reformers, in like manner, while aiming at a good end, do immense mischief in the attempt; and the amount of good they accomplish is very insignificant. Beware of such spirits! Cleave to those institutions which are sanctioned by the church of the living God. Nor must you suffer your zeal for society to lead you to neglect the duties of self-cultivation, and of making the companions of your domestic hearth happy. These are first duties. Fulfil their claims, and then do your utmost for the world without.

You may be called, by the force of circumstances, to travel from home, without the protection of a friend, to places in which you are totally unacquainted. There is danger in this, because of the numerous villains who lurk around large cities in search of prey; yet, with proper precautions, you may do so safely. You should always ascertain before going to a strange place where you are to stop. Nothing should induce you to go into a large city, utterly ignorant of the person or place you are to inquire for. To do so, is to throw yourself in the way of danger; for in all such places there are creatures whose souls are steeped in the deepest dyes of wickedness, ready to beguile the unwary into places of shame; as was the sad fate of a young lady I will name ALICE. Her connections were quite respectable, but, with a praiseworthy spirit of independence, she resolved to support herself by entering a cotton mill. Unfortunately for her happiness, she hastened to a certain city, without any previous knowledge of the place, or acquaintance with any of its inhabitants. She began to make inquiries of the persons who stood around the depot, when a well-dressed man stepped up and told her he was an agent for a corporation in a neighboring city, where her opportunities for self-support would be much superior. Pleased with his apparently disinterested manner, and scarcely knowing what else to do, she accepted his proposal to conduct her thither. He accompanied her to the place, and led her, — poor, deceived girl, — to a haunt of sorrow and sin, where, by dint of cruelty, threats and confinement, she became lost to virtue, to society, and to heaven!

Beware, therefore, young lady, of placing confidence in strangers! But beware still more of putting yourself in a situation where that confidence is necessary. A woman's helplessness is her danger, and she is never more helpless than when she enters a strange city, unknowing upon whom to call, or where to make it her home. Her sense of helplessness embarrasses her action, and points her out as a suitable person to be beguiled. On the contrary, if she knows her destination, she moves with confidence and ease; the vile dare not molest her if she acts with common prudence, and she is comparatively safe; though it is my opinion that unless she has gained experience by first travelling in company with others, a young lady ought not to travel alone, unless circumstances make it her absolute duty. In such a case, her safety must be secured by proper precaution and demeanor, and by a fitting trust in God, as her almighty protector and guardian.

Did you ever study that picture of the royal Hebrew melodist, which, with seeming unconsciousness, he drew of himself, in the third psalm? Absalom, his ingrate son, had driven him from his throne, and compelled him to maintain his kingly and paternal rights by an appeal to the sword. By various acts he had also succeeded in winning thousands of the bravest sons of Judah to join the standard of revolt. The weary old warrior was thereby placed in extremely perilous circumstances. He was a fugitive king, an injured and abused father, a strongly-tried sufferer. But, in the midst of this fierce storm of woes, behold him, at eventide, quietly reposing on his couch, and sleeping as calmly and sweetly as a babe slumbers on its mother's breast. With amiable simplicity he sung, "*I laid me down and slept!*"

Yes, he slept with the voices of unnatural war ringing in his ears! But how could he sleep amidst such sounds? Was he insensitive and stupidly resigned to his fate? Nay, he was keenly alive to his condition; but let him reveal the hidden philosophy of his slumbers, in his mournfully pleasant psalm. Hear him singing, "*I cried unto the Lord with my voice, and he heard me out of his holy hill!*"

FAITH IN GOD, you see, supported him. But for that, his strong soul would have sunk in deep waves of despairing sorrow. And what but such a TRUST in God, my dear young friend, can sustain you, when, leaving the home-world of your youth, you go out into society, to meet troops of dangers, and to combat with powerful enemies to your peace and safety? Poor, friendless, and desolate of heart, you will be without faith in Jesus. Turn your heart, then, to him, with tears of penitential love; and you may go out into the great world, singing,

> "What though a thousand hosts engage,
> A thousand worlds, my soul to shake;
> I have a shield shall quell their rage,
> And drive their alien armies back.
> Portrayed, it bears a bleeding Lamb;
> I dare believe in Jesus' name."

CHAPTER XI.

COURTSHIP AND MARRIAGE.

LADY, I wish you to study the beautiful image of mutual affection contained in the following lines:

> "Side by side we stood,
> Like two young trees, whose boughs in early strength
> Screen the weak saplings of the rising grove,
> And brave the storm together."

And now, behold yonder two heights, between which rolls a furious river! They are parted, and the "mining depths" so intervene that they can meet no more.

Can you believe that those loving trees with their infolded branches, and these jagged rocks with their dark torrents, are images of the same thing?

Widely as they contrast, they are, nevertheless, both equally fitting figures of the marriage state: the former of a happy, the latter of an unhappy marriage. In the first, kindred spirits, governing their hearts by mutual wisdom, are united in blissful and pleasing affection; in the second, two unmatched souls are held in hateful contiguity by a legal bond, but divided in heart by a torrent of passionate aversion.

If you are among the multitude who form their notions of love and marriage from sickly novels, from theatrical performances, and from flippant conversation, you probably question the correctness of my second figure. Marriage, to your uninstructed fancy, is a "seed of ineffable joy only. Its future is spread as a bright May day, and before your eyes golden years dance in bridal hours."

> "Thus, in the desert's dreary waste,
> By magic power produced in haste,
> As old romances say,
> Castles and groves, and music sweet,
> The senses of the trav'ler cheat,
> And stop him in his way.

But, while he gazes with surprise,
The charm dissolves, the vision dies,
'T was but enchanted ground."

Thus wil. your ideal of married life be changed into a wilderness by experience, unless it be entered upon with wisdom and precaution.

Marriage is a high and holy state, designed by its almighty Author to promote the health, happiness, purity and real greatness of our species. It is proper, therefore, for you to desire it, to prepare yourself for it, and to accept it, under fitting circumstances. It is equally improper for you to fancy that you cannot be truly happy in a single state, or to hastily accept the first offer that you may receive, lest you should never have a second. Better, far better, will it be for you to live and die unwedded, than to give your hand and person to one who is unsuited to your disposition, or unfitted, by bad habits, to make you a happy wife; or than to enter so responsible a relation without those mental and moral qualifications which are essential to its enjoyment. A single life is not without its advantages while a married one which fails of accomplishing its true end is the acme of earthly wretchedness. There is many a wife, who, having married incautiously and hastily, has buried even her hopes of happiness deep in a grave of despair; who sees nothing to cheer her in the future; whose silent sighings, had they a voice, would cry,

> "Mine after-life! What is mine after-life?
> My day is closed! the gloom of night is come!
> A hopeless darkness settles o'er my fate:
> My doom is closed!"

"How terrible!" you exclaim. Yes, it is terrible, indeed; but it is truth, — and it may be your experience, if you are not careful concerning the character of him you accept for your husband.

Marriage, properly viewed, is a union of kindred minds, — a blending of two souls in mutual, holy affection,—and not merely or chiefly a union of persons. Its physical aspects, pure and necessary as they are, are its lowest and least to be desired ones; indeed, they derive all their sanctity from the spiritual affinity existing between the parties. So emphatically is this the fact, that marriage without mutual affection is defilement and sin. Virtuous love alone can give dignity and innocency to the relation. Hence, the holy Scriptures enjoin husbands to "love their wives," and wives to "reverence their husbands," with the same authoritative voice as that with which they enjoin marriage itself.

These are the only views of this subject, young lady, that you can innocently entertain; and, in this light, it will not harm you in the least to reflect upon it. There are ideas, romantic, impassioned, immodest, derived from impure novels and impurer fancies, which you must prayerfully exclude from the chambers of your soul, or they will prepare you for the tempter, and lead you captive into an untimely marriage, if not into still deeper wretchedness. But those loftier conceptions of it will only stimulate you to cultivate those mental and moral qualities which will fit you to enjoy the state, and to the exercise of a calm judgment in the disposal of your affections.

Many young ladies indulge in very nonsensical

opinions, or, I should rather say, notions, concerning love. They foolishly fancy themselves bound to be "smitten," to "fall in love," to be "love-sick," with almost every silly idler who wears a fashionable coat, is tolerably good-looking, and pays them particular attention. Reason, judgment, deliberation, according to their fancies, have nothing to do with love. Hence, they yield to their feelings, and give their company to young men, regardless of warning advice or entreaty. A father's sadness, a mother's tears, are treated with contempt, and often with bitter retorts. Their lovers use flattering words, and, like silly moths fluttering round the fatal lamp, they allow themselves to be charmed into certain misery. Reader, beware of such examples; eschew such false notions! Learn that your affections are under your own control; that pure affection is founded upon esteem; that estimable qualities in a man can alone secure the continuance of connubial love; that if these are not in him, your love has no foundation, it is unreal, and will fall, a wilted flower, as soon as the excitement of youthful passion is overpast. Restrain your affections, therefore, with vigor; it will cost you far less pain to stifle them in their birth, than to languish through the years of woe which are inseparable from an unsuitable marriage.

If I am correct in my statements concerning love and marriage, the true idea of courtship is already obvious. What is it in its beginning, but an opportunity for the parties to ascertain their fitness for each other? What, in its progress, but a means of forming and strengthening that genuine affection, which is the true basis of marriage? With every young lady the paramount question concerning him who offers her particular attentions, ought to be, "Is he worthy of my love?" Her first aim should be to decide it. She should observe him well and thoughtfully, — study his character as it may be expressed in his countenance, his words, spirit, and actions. Through her parents she should inquire into his previous history, and learn especially IF HE HAS BEEN A DUTIFUL SON AND AN AFFECTIONATE BROTHER. This last is a vital test, though it is generally overlooked; but very sure I am, that a young man devoid of filial and fraternal love, will not, cannot make a good husband.

Now all this advice is perhaps lost upon my almost scornful reader. She thinks me a cold, calculating adviser, and perhaps pronounces me heartless. Be it so. Yet if she despises my counsel and marries an unworthy man, she will often turn back to it with remorseful reflections. Lady, mine is not a cold heart. I understand the ardor of youthful feeling, and comprehend all your difficulty in yielding to my instructions. Passion is strong in a young breast; it is often delirious — mad! It blinds the judgment, steels the conscience, bewilders the imagination, captivates the reason. Study its wild workings, as before a mirror, in the following words of Basil, a military chieftain, who, enthralled by a sudden affection for a beautiful woman, allowed himself to be detained with his troops from the field of battle, and thereby placed the fate of an empire in jeopardy. Hear him debating the opposing claims of duty and affection:

> "Well, there is yet one day of life before me,
> And, whatsoe'er betide, I will enjoy it.

Though but a partial sunshine in my lot,
I will converse with her, gaze on her still,
If all behind were pain and misery.
Pain! were it not the easing of all pain,
E'en in the dismal gloom of after years,
Such dear remembrance on the mind to wear,
Like silvery moonbeams on the nighted deep,
When heaven's blest sun is gone?"

Poor Basil! All his rhapsodical heroism evaporated a few hours afterwards, when he learned that he was disgraced by his commander-in-chief, for his absence from the battle-field, and, in a fit of furious despair, he rushed uncalled into eternity!

And it is ever thus. Passion leads us into a dream-land of folly. Time dissolves the airy fabric of the fancy, and the soul awakes to mourn, disconsolate, amid the ruins which surround it. Listen not, therefore, lady, to the voices of passion. Heed your reason. Keep the precious love of your young heart, until you find a man every way worthy of it. You have no treasure like that love. Bestow it unworthily, and you are hopelessly ruined. Give it to some manly heart, full of noble qualities, and you will drink joy from a pure fountain. If no such heart seeks it, then let it remain in your own breast, reserved for heaven alone. Say of your love,

> "It is
> The invaluable diamond, which I give
> Freely away, or else, forever hid,
> Must bury — like the noble-hearted merchant,
> Who, all unmoved by the Rialto's gold
> Or king's displeasure, to the mighty sea
> Gave back his pearl — too proud to part with it
> Below its price."

The human "heart is deceitful above all things," says its great Creator. Perhaps it is never more inclined to conceal itself than in the intercourse of the sexes. Duplicity, to some extent, is almost universal in courtship. Hence follows the necessity of the utmost caution on the part of a young lady, in admitting a lover to her confidence. The value she places on her purity must be very trifling, if she admits a stranger, however plausible his manners, or however specious his pretences, to the sacred intimacy of courtship, without some unquestionable assurances of his morality and respectability. He may wear the garb of a gentleman, he may use the most courteous language, he may profess the utmost regard for virtue, and yet be a villain! Be wary, therefore, of an entire stranger, who professes to admire you. Demand references, ascertain his principles, study watchfully his spirit. A man soon exhibits his real self in the interchange of thought; and the chief reason why so many women are cheated by seducers, is because they are not sufficiently anxious to know the true characters of the men who flatter them. If they were, the hollow hypocrisy of passion would betray itself to their cautious minds, as shown by COLERIDGE:

"Soft the glances of the youth,
Soft his speech and soft his sigh;
But no sound like simple truth,
But no true love in his eye."

So, also, a man filled with generous and honorable love will make his soul most visible when most unguarded. He is like young TRACY DE VERE, in ELIZA COOK's poem:

"There's a halcyon smile spread o'er his face,
Shedding a calm and radiant grace;

> There 's a sweetness of sound in his talking tones,
> Betraying the gentle spirit he owns."

But if, instead of watching to detect character, a young woman tolerates the utterance of sentiments and the manifestation of a spirit from which her moral sense secretly recoils, — if she permits the unholy word, the passionate glance, to pass unrebuked and unresented, — if she persuades herself that these displays of a wicked mind are foibles she must consent to endure in order to become a wife, — she rushes blindfold into the wolf's den, and becomes a willing partner in effecting her own ruin. But if she herself wears the impenetrable armor of mental and moral purity, — if she is resolved to wed only with a good and virtuous man, — if her heart be unspotted, and if it shines with the dazzling splendor of holy affection, — a false-hearted man, a hypocritical pretender to her affection, will soon flee from her society, convinced that his case is absolutely hopeless. This thought is most beautifully presented in the following description of a pure-minded girl, — a model for all her sex:

"Impure desire
Round that chaste light but hovered to expire;
Her angel nature found its own defence
E'en in the instincts of its innocence;
As that sweet flower which opens every hue
Of its frank heart to eyes content to view,
But folds its leaves and shrinks in sweet disdain
From the least touch that would the bloom profane.
O'er all the woman did the virgin reign,
And love the heart might break — it could not stain."

The man whom you accept as your suitor should, therefore, be pure-minded, sincere, and spotless in his moral character. He should be a *self-denying man;* rejecting the wine-cup, tobacco, and all other forms of intemperance; if any single vice acts the tyrant over him, it is not safe to intrust your happiness to his keeping. He should be an *energetic man,* or he will sink in seas of difficulty, and drag you down to cavernous depths of sorrow. He should possess *a cultivated intellect,* otherwise he will either keep you in obscurity, or subject you to incessant mortification by his ignorance. He should be *industrious;* if he is a drone, he will pluck down ruin on your habitation. He must be *economical;* a spendthrift husband will sow the field of your after-life with the seed of unknown struggles and trials,—with thorns and briars. He must be *benevolent*, since a covetous man, who sacrifices his own soul at the shrine of the gold demon, will not hesitate to immolate your happiness on the same accursed altar. He must not be a *proud man;* for pride is always cruel, selfish, remorseless. He should not be *clownish* on the one hand, nor *foppish* on the other, because a stupid clown and a conceited fop are alike mortifying to the sensibilities of every woman of good sense. He should not be deformed or badly defeatured; I do not say he must needs be handsome, for beauty is far from being necessary to goodness, yet he should not be repulsive; if he is so, your heart will recoil from him. Above all things, he ought to be *religious.* No man's character is reliable, if his virtues are not founded on reverence and love for his Creator. How can he be depended upon to be faithful to wife or children, who despises the loftier claims of his God? It is true that many irreligious men are kind, indulgent, and affectionate to their families; nevertheless, they are in constant danger of falling away from the conventional virtue which is their only adornment. The pure gold of real goodness is not in the hearts of men who fear not God. A young lady ought to be afraid to unite her destiny with a man who makes daring but fatal war on Jehovah! She who does so risks all that is precious to a woman in both worlds. Therefore I exhort my reader to "MARRY ONLY IN THE LORD."

Should you be addressed by a young man who combines these excellences, you may rightly encourage his attentions, after consulting your parents, *especially your mother*. The habit of concealing matters of affection from a parent is not only dangerous, but wicked. There may be exceptions to this statement, I know, for there are women, — no, female monsters! they are not true women, — who hold their daughters for sale to the highest bidder. They wish them to marry fortunes, not husbands; they would wed them to rank and station, not to worthy, loving hearts. They would send them to unsanctified bridal chambers, where the absence of pure spiritual affection insures their defilement, by excluding the true spirit and higher ends of marriage. Shame! shame! on such unwomanly mothers. My reader, thank God, is not cursed with such an one. They are found chiefly among the heartless worshippers of fashion. Your mother is, most likely, a true woman. She has a mother's heart. She seeks to secure your best interests. Consult her, then, in these matters of the heart. She will advise you wisely, prudently, safely. Even if she has imprudently indulged you, her maternal instinct will judge acutely of the man who asks her daughter's love. Beware how you slight her opinions! Should you be already listening to the bewitching whispers of a youth from whose presence your mother shrinks with fear, gaze a moment on the etching I will now lay before you.

There was a lady who had two graceful, accomplished daughters. The eldest, — call her MYRA, — was addressed by a very prepossessing young man. He had talents, opportunities, and connections, but he had vices also. He was a lover of wine. With many a word of entreaty, with tears, the mother of Myra besought her to refuse his attentions. Myra met her affectionate labors by exclaiming, in the most unfilial spirit, "I am determined to receive his visits."

Finding persuasion to be vain, her mother exercised her authority, and forbade the young man to enter her house. Myra was obstinate and wicked; deprived of his visits, she corresponded with him, eloped with him, married him. Trampling on her mother's wisdom, she followed the bent of her inclinations, and scornfully triumphed over all restraints, as she walked proudly by her husband's side.

Alas, her triumph was very short! A few days after their marriage, her husband came home intoxicated. From that hour her doom of misery was sealed. Abuse, poverty, degradation, rags, wretchedness, became her heritage. Her hopes were all quenched in bitter tears; her unfilial conduct was terribly rewarded by years of unspeakable remorse. May her example excite you to record a solemn purpose to be guided by a parent's wisdom, and to be married, if possible, with a parent's smile. Sweet is a parent's kiss, when it approvingly touches the lips of a daughter in the bridal hour. On the contrary, that bridal day is dark which has its sun obscured by the shadow of a parent's frown.

Having a parent's approval, and a kindred spirit for a suitor, you still need to cultivate caution in the intimacies of courtship. While you avoid all coquettishness of spirit, you must also guard against too much freedom. Be frank, simple, trustful in your intercourse, but avoid all boldness on your own part, and shrink from the least approach to impropriety on his. Do not permit your lover to remain in your company later than ten o'clock in the evening; it ought to make a young lady blush even to listen to a proposal to sit up all, or nearly all, night, — an ancient practice, which, I am pleased to know, is becoming unfashionable. I condemn it, because it is wrong, and disgraces the parties in their own estimation, as well as in the opinion of all virtuous persons. Your conversation ought also to be seasoned with common sense. All mere soft, silly talk about love should be discarded by sensible young persons. You and your suitor are not silly children, but intelligent and immortal minds. You do not meet to sigh and look foolish at each other, but to grow into a high and holy unity of mind and heart; and your intercourse should be governed by this exalted purpose.

Do not be in haste to marry. I favor early, but not premature marriages. A girl of sixteen or eighteen is unfitted in every respect to enter on this state. Her physical organization, her mind, her moral character, are alike unripe for it, and will involve her in a net-work of pains, trials, and griefs, of which she has little conception. No young lady, except under very extraordinary circumstances, should wed before she is twenty, and twenty-two is a still better age. Wait, then, my young friend, however solicitous your betrothed may be to consummate your engagements. Bid him improve his circumstances, cultivate his intellect, and lay sure and broad foundations for your future happiness. Thus, doing all that human prudence dictates, diligently studying the will of God, you may rationally expect the divine blessing to fall upon you, and to abide with you through the tangled paths of your earthly life.*

And now, my young friend, I bid you an affectionate farewell. I have given you such hints and counsels as my experience in the ways of mankind suggested. I have the fullest confidence in the fitness of my advice. I lay down my pen, delightfully conscious that if you give due heed to these pages, they will add to your enjoyment, and improve your character. Fail not, therefore, to attempt the paths of duty. Achieve the victories of virtue! Seize the crown of a holy life, and remember that all true strength of character has its foundation in faith. It is by believing the truth that human hearts are purified from sin, fitted for the struggles of life, and raised to fellowship with God. When the woman, whose wasting disease had reduced her to poverty, to melancholy, and to weariness, moved by a divine

* For counsels to the married, see the author's book entitled "Bridal Greetings," &c.

confidence in her heart, which assured her that if she could only touch the hem of the Saviour's garment her disorder would disappear, put forth her hand, in that instant a healing virtue went forth from Christ, and renewed her trembling body. Divine power followed human trust. It is ever thus with those who seek the gifts of God. No sooner does a human being bring a scriptural promise, and, with humility and contrition, ask God to fulfil it, — not doubting but that it is then and there fulfilled, — than God immediately imparts his grace, and continues to do so as long as the soul believes. TO BELIEVE GOD, and TO BELIEVE IN GOD, under all the circumstances of life, are the steps that lead infallibly to a pure life on earth and to a blissful eternity after death; and there, dangers, trials, fears, and sorrows will never intrude their shadows to disturb the happy inmates, but "GOD SHALL WIPE AWAY ALL TEARS FROM THEIR EYES; AND THERE SHALL BE NO MORE DEATH, NEITHER SORROW, NOR CRYING; NEITHER SHALL THERE BE ANY MORE PAIN, FOR THE FORMER THINGS ARE PASSED AWAY!"

www.ingramcontent.com/pod-product-compliance
Lightning Source LLC
LaVergne TN
LVHW050515100826
845148LV00002B/338

* 9 7 8 1 4 2 5 5 2 1 4 4 8 *